The Book of Twitter

AF873534

How To Get 100,000+ Followers On Twitter And What To Do With Them After You've Got Them

The Book of Twitter

How To Get 100,000+ Followers On Twitter And What To Do With Them After You've Got Them

Heilan Yvette Grimes

Hollow Earth Publishing

The Book of Twitter
How To Get 100,000+ Followers On Twitter And What To Do With Them After You've Got Them

ISBN-10: 1879196042 ISBN-13: 978-1-879196-04-9

First electronic edition July 2011

20 19 18 17 16 15 14 13 12 11 10 9 8 7 6 5 4 3 2 1

Colophon: The Cover, Half Title, Title, are set in Aller Display and Aller. Section/Chapter Openings are all set in Gill Sans Bold. The text is set in 12/14 Gill Sans x 45.

The cover was produced using TwBg (see page 158).

Hollow Earth Publishing
PO Box 51480 • Boston, MA 02205-1480
TheBookofTwitter.com

Dedicated to the fine people at Twitter
without whom this book would really not be possible.

(And this dedication in no way implies endorsement
of any kind by Twitter of this book.)

Also

Thank you Lee Dolby, who on April 17, 2008, showed me something on his cellphone called Twitter. Couldn't think what it's possible use could be, but to be polite, I opened an account after he helpfully showed me where I should go to create an account.

TABLE OF CONTENTS

FOREWORD

HOW TO KEEP THIS BOOK UP-TO-DATE

Twitter is many things. It's fun, it's a micro-blogging platform, it's a way to promote yourself or your business. This book teaches you all about Twitter and how to use it to get followers, and promote yourself or your business, or to just have fun.

Twitter is a rapidly changing environment. Most of the websites listed in this book did not exist a year ago. Quite a few of them won't exist a year from now. They'll be replaced by newer, better websites.

One-Year Subscription to Keep This Book Up-to-Date

I consider this book a work in progress. I will make changes to reflect new techniques and ideas on how to use Twitter. I'll add new interesting websites and delete defunct websites, In short, I intend to keep this book current.

I'm going to do this by offering a one-year subscription to at first a regular email with changes, suggestions, twitterers whose followers have a high followback percentage, free statistics/tracking templates, etc. And if there are enough changes in the book, a new free download of the book. Eventually there will be a private website (TheBookofTwitter.com). Right now the first page of this website is an order page for this book, and a $10 subscription order form for a one-year update and suggestions to complement the book. I am currently working on a login and password protected area with forums, suggestions, and links to interesting Twitterstreams and websites. Anyone subscribing to the current $10 extras will automatically be included in the private website.

I will be blogging on the website about how to use Twitter, including how to integrate it in marketing and promotional campaigns and go into specifics that I can't go into in this book.

There will be a forum for readers to exchange their views and ideas. And I'll be there to help answer your questions, and give you encouragement and suggestions when you feel your Twitter account just isn't going right.

I will also be listing [twitter_id]'s of twitterers whose followers followback. Some that have an almost 85% followback percentage. You should be able to increase your followers by just following the twitterers I list.

But, as I've said, you're better off with targeted followers and I'll give you lots of suggestions to find them.

If the book changes appreciably, then I'll give you a new link to download an updated version of The Book of Twitter.

All of the above is only $10 per year subscription. And I think you'll find it quite valuable. Read more at TheBookofTwitter.com.

Become an Affiliate and Sell The Book of Twitter

If you'd like to sell this book I will set you up with your own squeeze page and PayPal link. All you have to do is promote that link and you will receive a commission on any sales through that link. The ebook sells for $10 and I'll give you $2 commission on each book you sell. Additionally, if someone signs up for the 1-year book update and information subscription, you'll get $2 of that. So, your potential for each book you sell is $4. And I'll make it incredibly easy for you by providing you a link to your own free internet squeeze page.

If you're interested or have any questions about becoming an affiliate please may contact me at yvettegr@hotmail.com, or signup at TheBookofTwitter.com.

PREFACE

FOCUS OF THIS BOOK

This book is about more than just showing you how to get lots of followers on Twitter. That's actually fairly easy. But having a lot of followers means nothing if you don't know what to do with them.

I'm going to teach you how to set up and use Twitter for your business, or personal success. You might want to make money using Twitter; or you might want to use it to help people or charities; manage a project; or simply keep in contact with others. This book will give you suggestions on unique ways to use Twitter.

I'm not going to go into a lot of specifics about eMarketing and eCommerce, though I'll touch on those topics a little bit. However, I do have another book coming out which will deal specifically with how to use Twitter, facebook, other social media sites, and blogs in your eCommerce eMarketing, and eBlasts.

This book is a work in progress. Twitter is changing all the time so this book is going to be updated continuously. You can subscribe to get updates and useful suggestions every month for one year at a nominal $10 price (see page xvii).

If you have any corrections or suggestions to this book, please don't hesitate to contact me. If there's something you want me to add, let me know. If you have any questions, let me know.

DISCLAIMER

Although the techniques I describe in this book have worked for me, I cannot guarantee they will work for you since I don't know exactly how you're using them. If used incorrectly you could get your account suspended. I make no claims you will in any way have success with these techniques, because I have no way of knowing if you're following the techniques as I describe them.

Also, though I have a Twitter account and love Twitter, I am in no way affiliated with Twitter professionally. I wish them the greatest of success, though, and think Twitter is awesome.

If you have any questions, comments, suggestions, etc., please do not hesitate to contact me. I'm always willing to help.

Heilan Yvette Grimes
yvettegr@hotmail.com

CHAPTER 1

WHAT IS TWITTER?

HOW TO USE THIS BOOK

This book is not a narrative so you don't have to start at page one and read linearly. You can hop around, go to sections which interest you right now, read a little bit, then go to another section. Use the book to answer the questions you have right now.

There are a lot of websites listed throughout this book. I do check to make certain websites are still active. But, websites come and go all the time and I can't guarantee that every link leads to an active website. However, if I find an inactive link because the website has shut down, well try to find a replacement website and update the book.

If you have an eBook version of this book all the page references to other pages in the book (i.e.,see page _ _ _ – this is an example, not an actual reference, so it is not hotlinked) are active hotlinks. Click on the "see page _ _ _" and you'll be taken to that page. Clicking on a website URL opens your default browser and takes you to that website. If you roll over a word and your cursor turns into a hand then the word you're hovering over is hotlinked either to another page in this book or a website. Clicking on it will take you to the reference link or website.

[TWITTER_ID]

When you see [twitter_id] used in a reference in this book and are told to replace it with an id (or username), don't use the brackets when you replace it. For example to replace twitter.com/[twitter_id] with your id (using my id as an example):

RIGHT: twitter.com/yvettegr   WRONG: twitter.com/[yvettegr]

WHAT IS TWITTER?

Obviously you've heard of Twitter or you wouldn't have bought this book. But have you thought about what Twitter actually is?

Opinions vary. Some people think it's the greatest thing since sliced bread. Other people think of it as a worthless waste of time; a giant vacuum cleaner sucking away hours of their life.

But practically, Twitter is a micro-blogging platform. If you think a regular blog is too time-consuming, and maybe you don't really have that much to say, then Twitter is a platform in which you can get your ideas out in short increments. It integrates well as a feed with your regular blog or facebook page, or as a separate RSS feed.

The really great thing about Twitter is its immediacy. A tweet goes out and people read it immediately, can retweet it, can respond to it, all within seconds.

WHY ONLY 140 CHARACTERS PER TWEET?

Tweets are short, no more than 140-characters long. The 140-character limit has a reason. Data is sent over the internet in small packets via many pathways. This is called packet switching. Packet switching keeps the internet pathways from clogging up with huge files. Say you have a 100mb file. That's a really large file. If it were to go all at once it might clog up a pathway while it makes its way to its destination, slowing down everything behind it.

Think of it this way. You've got one huge package to carry down a hallway that's just as wide as the package. Everyone else carrying smaller packages behind you can't get around you so all those other packages have to slow down and begin getting backed up. They have to wait until there are other hallways they can turn onto and take different paths to their destinations. The alternate paths might be longer than following behind you, but because they don't have to wait for you, their packages arrive more quickly at theirs destinations. But, until people behind you can get to alternate hallways they're backed up and going only as fast as you're going.

There is a solution. What if you took everything out of your big package and made lots of smaller packages that you and several others could carry agreeing to eventually meet at a restaurant several blocks away? Then you could run down one corridor and pass those packages moving more slowly (as long as they weren't large enough to block your way). People carrying the other packages could run down different hallways. And even faster packages can pass you. If everyone is going in the same direction and things slow down you can take another hallway, even going outside, and eventually all of you arrive at the restaurant by lots of different paths. Some will get there before you, some after. But once you all get there you can put your small packages back into a big box. That's how packets on the internet work.

The internet breaks up files into small packets. Each packet has a header saying what file it's attached to. If it's the start of a file the header says there's nothing to attach before it but it has a footer telling which file comes after it. Other files have headers and footers saying what file they go after and what file goes after them. The final file packet in a file says I go after this file and nothing comes after. I'm the last packet in the file put us all together. All the packets contain information on where they're going. So that 100 mb file is broken up into packets which eventually arrive at their same destination where they are put back together.

Let's pretend the destination is a friend of yours across town in Boston. The first packet of your message begins it's journey and finds the quickest path takes it to Houston, Chicago, back to Boston and eventually to your friends email box. Other packets also see that's the quickest path so they take that path too, although at Chicago instead of going to Boston some might head over to Los Angeles because going directly back to Boston was clogged but Los Angeles to Boston was clear. The path the files had taken, because it was the quickest had filled up and slowed down because of increased traffic. Meanwhile another packet can't follow the first packet because that path is now slow. It finds just going to Portsmouth, NH, and then back down to Boston is the fastest path. Then that path because it was the fastest starts getting clogged and slows down. Another packet finds its fasted path is to head over to Phoenix, then to Boise, and finally to your friend's email box in Boston. And so it goes. Quick paths fill up and slow down. Slow paths clear up and become quicker. Then they get slower, etc.

Every packet finds its own fastest path to get to your friend's email box. Then all the packets are joined together and your friend gets just one message. Breaking files up into small packets makes the internet work faster since none of the packets have to wait for a really huge file to lumber it's way along the path and possibly block a path.

What does this have to do with Twitter's 140-character limit? That's about as large as you can get with a message without it having to be broken into packets. Tweets don't have to be broken up and sent along different pathways and then joined when they reach their destination. They all reach the same destination. Since twitterers are sending out hundreds of millions of tweets each day, not having to break them into packets saves Twitter a lot of time and bandwidth. Makes it pretty much the most efficient messaging system around.

WHY HAVE YOU DECIDED TO SIGN UP FOR AN ACCOUNT ON TWITTER?

Figuring out why you've signed up for Twitter and how you want to use Twitter will help you send interesting tweets and gain an audience. Remember to tweet softly but carry a big stick.

Suggested Uses for Twitter

- Fun
- Marketing

- Keeping up privately with family and friends
- Promoting your business
- Showing how interesting you are
- Being helpful to others
- Educating others
- Being political
- Tweeting about your faith
- Sharing information about your hobby
- Book reviews
- Movie reviews
- Jokes
- Quotes
- Coordinating an event
- Keeping people informed about an upcoming event
- Letting the world know about your upcoming (birthday, wedding, vasectomy, vacation)
- Maybe you're coping with a rough patch in your life and want to share it with others to help them and get feedback that might help you?

Are you on Twitter just for fun? Do you want to learn or teach others about your hobby? Maybe you like movies and want to post mini-reviews? Or how about suggesting good books to read? Do you want to promote your business, or yourself? Have you written a book you want to promote? Do you have a company you want to promote? Are you selling things over the internet, maybe on eBay, and want to mention them with a link to your shopping site or eBay listing? Or, maybe you just want to connect with friends and family with private tweets which only they can see?

All of the above are legitimate uses for Twitter. Some users want to build up a huge following. Others just want to send and receive private tweets between family and friends, and have only a few followers. And, you can always have multiple accounts. One that's private for friends and family; others that promote your business or hobby. You can have as many Twitter accounts as you want. And they're all free.

TWITTER CAN INTEGRATE WITH YOUR OTHER SOCIAL NETWORKING SITES

Posting Your Tweets to Your Blog

There are many Twitter/blog integration tools so your tweets automatically show up as a feed on your blog. Just google "posting tweets to my blog" and you'll find a lot of suggestions, programs, and directions.

There are also other methods of posting to your blog, including an RSS feed (described below).

Tweetremote

tweetremote.com

TweetRemote relies on you using the hashtags #text, #link, #image, in your tweet (see page 79 for more about hashtags). This makes your tweet look a little strange but let's TweetRemote pull in the tweet to your blog. It also means if you don't want to mirror a tweet on your blog, you just leave off the hashtags and TweetRemote ignores that tweet. So, you do have some control. Most RSS feeders feed all of your tweets to your blog. Sometimes you may not want to do that.

TweetRemote does require that you setup some code on your own blog. So, you have to have a little knowledge about html.

Wordpress.com/Buddypress.com, Blogger, LiveJournal

If you host your blog on Wordpress, or install Wordpress or Buddypress on your website, then mirroring your twitterstream to your blog is much easier. All you have to do is search for a Twitter plugin, install and activate it to receive your twitterstream. You can also search for an RSS feed reader, select the plugin you think will work best with your blog and install and activate it.

You can search for equivalent plugins to install and activate for Blogger, LiveJournal, Drupal, Joomla, etc.

LINKING YOUR TWITTER PAGE TO FACEBOOK

This is incredibly easy to do. Follow this link:

http://Twitter.com/goodies/widgets

LINKING YOUR FACEBOOK PAGE TO TWITTER

This is incredibly easy to do. Follow this link:

https://www.facebook.com/Twitter

CREATING AN RSS FEED OF YOUR TWEETS

RSS stands for Real Simple Syndication. It's an easy way to create feeds of your blog posts, facebook posts, or tweets and feed them wherever you want. An RSS feed contains metadata such as the date and author of the post. You'll see your entire tweet in your feed. However, if you have long blog/website posts you might want to summarize and send only a portion in your RSS feed.

There are many ways to create RSS feeds of your tweets. Here are several.

Twitter

Without question the easiest is to use the RSS feed generator at the bottom of the Twitter sidebar. It will only work if you click on your Profile page rather than the Home page in the top menu. The Home page reads "RSS feed", the Profile page reads "RSS feed of [twitter_id]".

Click on the orange RSS feed button and Twitter creates a feed with the options in the sidebar of choosing All, Today, Last Seven Days, This Month, or Last Month.If you have a lot of tweets and select All, then it'll take a little bit of time to generate your feed.

You can sort your tweets by Date, Title, Source, or New. You can also Mail a Link of the page, Subscribe to have your tweets sent to you (or anyone else) via email. You can bookmark the results and place them in your bookmarks menu so you can easily bring up your RSS feed any time you want by clicking on the bookmark.

You can also copy the URL and use it as a hotlink address on a webpage or in a word processing document.

You'll notice each tweet has a "Read more..." at the end of the tweet. Click on this and the tweet will be shown individually as an html page with a link you can copy and paste if you want to just send that tweet to others.

Twitter Favorites

http://twitter.com/favorites/[twitter_id].rss

Change the [twitter_id] to your own [twitter_id] in the above and create your RSS feed directly from Twitter. For example, my RSS feed would be http://twitter.com/favorites/yvettegr.rss. This is probably the easiest way. You can then embed this URL in Google Reader or other RSS feed readers, as well as on your blog/website.

Twitterfeed

twitterfeed.com

This website creates RSS feeds from your Twitter (and facebook) accounts. Extremely easy to use and free. Just register (or sign in if you've already registered) and follow the simple steps to create your feed.

Step 1. Name your feed. Type the URL for your feed into the "Blog URL or RSS Feed URL".

Step 2. Configure where you want your feed to appear. Your options are Twitter, Statusnet, Heliotxt, or facebook. Obviously you can't send your twitterstream back to Twitter. However you could post it to the other services. Likewise if you had created a facebook feed, you could post that to Twitter.

You also have the option of creating various filters and can select which link shortener you want to use.

When you click back on Step 1 you'll see that the feed URL has changed and now says http://Twitter.com/statuses/user_timeline/{a series of numbers which reference your feed}.rss. You can copy this URL and use it on your blog to have your feed show up there or paste it into various feedreaders. If you just paste the URL into your browser you'll get a list of your most recent tweets.

Reader2Twitter

reader2twitter.appspot.com

Sync your Google Reader shared items to Twitter.

WANT TO MAKE A BOOK OF YOUR TWEETS?

Eventually, you're going to have a lot of tweets. Why not make them into a book? Here's a terrific site that'll generate a very nice-looking PDF ebook of your tweets:

http://tweetbook.in/tweetbook.php

SO YOU HAVE ABSOLUTELY NO IDEA WHAT TO TWEET!

In general, be interesting, be funny, be helpful. Point people to other twitterers and to other interesting tweets. If you find someone really interesting suggest to people they follow that person (make certain you're following them too). It's about community. Do you help your neighbor? You do if you want to be a good neighbor and be well-liked in the neighborhood. And it's fun.

Fortunately, there are lots of Twitter apps to give you helpful suggestions about tweets.

Trends24

http://trends24.appb.in

Trends 24 is particularly nice, listing the latest Twitter trends. So you can join in the conversation about the most popular trends happening on Twitter in the last few minutes, 1 hour ago, 2 hours ago, or 3 hours ago, 4 hours ago, up to a day ago. And you can break down those trends by country, or locally.

But, before you can tweet anything you have to set up your account which I will discuss in the next chapter.

CHAPTER 2

How to Open and Set up Your Twitter Account

WHAT'S IN A NAME?

Your [twitter_id] is how people will know you and find you on Twitter. Make your name unique, but not so unique no one will get it or search for it incorrectly. Take some time to come up with just the right name. It should be short (the shorter the better), descriptive, and memorable. But don't make it so short that it's indecipherable. If your name is too long people will have a difficult time responding to you since your name will be included in the 140-character Twitter limit. If someone responds back to one of your tweets they have to put

@[twitter_id]

at the beginning of their tweet so Twitter knows to whom to send the response. And if it's a DM (Direct Message – private message) they have to put:

DM @[twitter_id]

They only have 140-characters for all this. Say you love coin collecting and pick the name I_Love_Coin_Collecting. Someone tweeting you would send:

@I_Love_Coin_Collecting I love coin collecting too. Why don't we talk?

The above uses 24 (including the space after the [twitter_id] of your 140-character limit just for your address.

If they want to send you a DM it would use up 27 of your 140-character limit:

DM @I_Love_Coin_Collecting I love coin collecting too. Why don't we talk?

A better name might be @luvcoins which uses 10 characters giving you 14 (or 17 if it's a DM) extra characters for your message (over 10% more characters for your message:

@lovcoins I love coin collecting too. Why don't we talk?

But you can shorten @I_Love_Coin_Collecting even further. Twitter is not case specific, so you can use upper and lower case letters to define words rather than using the _ (underscore) to denote a space. You have to use the _ (underscore) because you can't use a blank space in a name. The reason is obvious. When Twitter comes to a blank space it thinks a word has ended. If you're using multiple words in your [twitter_id] Twitter won't recognize anything as part of your name after the first space. For example:

@I love coin collecting

Twitter would only see "@I" as your [twitter_id] and "love coin collecting" as part of your message. A space starts a new word. If it didn't Twitter wouldn't know how to end your [twitter_id].

You could use:

@I_love_coin_collecting

However the underscores add three extra characters to your name. This is better:

@ILoveCoinCollecting

Use upper and lower case to define words since upper or lower case doesn't matter in your [twitter_id]. However, a shorter name is even better.

BE UNIQUE

If your name is very common (i.e., JohnSmith) chances are it's already taken. If not, and you manage to snag it, you're going to be constantly confused for someone/something else. Make your name unique and marketable.

Think of your [twitter_id] as part of your overall branding on the Internet. That's why, if possible, you should be consistent on Twitter, YouTube, facebook, LinkedIn, your email, etc.

If you are already branded on other platforms (facebook, YouTube, LinkedIn, etc.) then try to have the same branding on Twitter. Consistency works. Most people misquote Emerson as "Consistency is the hobgoblin of little minds." The actual quote is "A foolish consistency is the hobgoblin of little minds". Consistent branding across social networks is good.

YOU DON'T HAVE TO BE YOU

You don't have to use your own name in your [twitter_id]. Instead of branding yourself maybe you want to use your Twitter account to tell jokes, post inspirational quotes, review movies or books, etc. Maybe you want to give health/diet tips, or tell people how to fix things around the house. You don't really need to put your name on that kind of twitterstream. In fact it's better if you come up with a [twitter_id] that reflects what you want to do with your twitterstream. @autojunkie for someone interested in restoring old cars is better than just @johnsmith. If your twitterstream is informational then your [twitter_id] should reflect that. However, if you're trying to promote yourself as an expert on the topics your tweeting about, then you will want to associate your name with your [twitter_id].

CORRESPONDING EMAIL ADDRESS

Another thing to consider is the email account you associate with your [twitter_id]. I try to make certain my email address matches my [twitter_id]. This makes it easier for people to remember.

The account I'm going to create in this chapter is "twitter.com/norsemyths", which was available. I tried to get norsemyths@me.com, norsemyths@hotmail.com, norsemyths@yahoo.com, norsemyths@aol.com, and norsemyths@gmail.com. All were taken. But, I really wanted my email address to match my Twitter account. Then I remembered in addition to hotmail.com Microsoft has their live.com email addresses. These are fairly new and not as filled up as the other major email clients. Sure enough norsemyths@live.com was available. So I was able to get an email address which mirrors the [twitter_id] I was going to create.

WHAT TWITTER WON'T LET YOU DO

Twitter has a few rules concerning [twitter_id]'s. First, you cannot put Twitter in your [twitter_id]. It will be rejected. Twitter realizes most people who see the word Twitter in a [twitter_id] will assume it's associated with Twitter. Since you aren't associated with Twitter, don't expect them to let you use their trademarked name.

WHAT TWITTER DISCOURAGES

Twitter allows names with words and phrases like "follow", "followback", "ifollowback", etc., but they don't look too kindly on them. They keep an extra special eye on [twitter_id]'s like that, and the first time you violate Twitter's TOS (Terms of Service) they yank the account.

Twitter also discourages anything that reeks of spam or get rich quick schemes. And if you actually do send spam Twitter will delete you immediately. Get rich quick schemes are a grayer area. Twitter does encourage people to use Twitter for their businesses. So they are somewhat tolerant of offers to make money through a company. But, if they start getting complaints or they investigate and see a get rich quick scheme they'll yank the account.

MORE SUGGESTIONS ON CHOOSING YOUR [TWITTER_ID]

Putting a Year in Your Name

It's not a very good idea to associate a year with your [twitter_id]. Tempus fugit. Twitter.com/johnsmith2011 might sound current now, but time doesn't stand still and it's not going to sound so current in 2016. True, you aren't locked into your [twitter_id] and can change it. But, if you make yourself JohnSmith2011 someone else might have beat you to JohnSmith2012. People also might assume you'll upgrade your name to the New Year each year. They might look for JohnSmith2012 and find someone completely opposite from you. JohnSmith2011 might be the sweetest guy in the world and everyone wants to be his friend. JohnSmith2012 might be rather notorious, crude, lewd, and socially unacceptable. You can avoid this by creating a name that doesn't age.

Avoid 0 for O

So you sell a wine called White Wolf and find Twitter.com/WhiteWolf is taken by a company making winter parkas. In a flash of inspiration you think, "What about Twitter.com/WhiteW0lf?" Instead of the letter "O" you'll use a "0" (zero). Bad idea. Everyone is going to forget you're WhiteW0lf (zero) and type in WhiteWolf (o). All your advertising efforts will result in your driving all your business to WhiteWolf. Think of something else. You want your name to be memorable, not something people have to think about to remember.

Okay, What About Using a Double Letter?

Twitter.com/WhiteW0lf didn't work out. So what if you use a double letter: Twitter.com/WhiiteWolf? Did you catch it? Look closely, there are two i's in WhiiteWolf. People will forget that. And they'll mistakenly type in WhiteWolf instead of WhiiteWolf and, again, you'll send all your business elsewhere. And don't forget the power of autocorrect. You may train some people to type WhiiteWolf, but then you'll be defeated by autocorrect, which will change it to WhiteWolf.

The Confusion of ter/tor

Don't use a confusing [twitter_id] that's easily misspelled. Names that end in "ter" and "tor" are often misspelled. Learn from the lesson of AT&T. Years ago they offered a dialup yellowpages/whitepages service. All you had to do to find the number for an individual or business was dial 1-800-operator and a friendly voice would answer and help you. AT&T spent millions of dollars advertising this service. That was millions of dollars advertising a service in which people had to punch in one of the most misspelled words in the English language. Their competitor MCI (later WorldCom, later gone bust and bankrupt) realized this and bought 1-800-operater and started their own yellow pages/whitepages service. So AT&T spent millions promoting a service, and the people liked the idea, but couldn't spell worth beans, and called 1-800-operater instead of 1-800-operator. AT&T eventually pulled the service.

So make certain your [twitter_id] is easy to spell.

Don't Vampire Off of Celebrities or Brand Names

Don't select a name that looks suspicious, tries to imitate a celebrity, or is associated with a brand. A lot of people who do this do it so they can spam other twitterers.

There are many reasons not to base your [twitter_id] on a celebrity. First and foremost is the celebrity probably doesn't like it. So, you are in no way ingratiating yourself to that celebrity. And building up a name based on a celebrity might be embarrassing if that celebrity implodes in scandal and you no longer like him/her.

If you do build a following and vampire off a celebrities' name all you're doing is limiting your followers to just those interested in that celebrity. You can't be justinbieber (he's justinbieber), nor is it a good idea to be justinbieber2. Why would anyone follow you? And what if you stop liking Justin Bieber? I know you think that'll never happen. But, David Cassidy doesn't have as many fans as he did a long time ago.

If you do happen to get a celebrities' moniker before they do, all they have to do is request Twitter give them the account. And unless your name is the same as the celebrities' Twitter will give the celebrity the account. You'll waste a lot of time building an account that will be taken away from you.

Stay away from brand names. They're usually trademarked and companies protect their trademarks. You'll be shut down rather quickly if you put Coca-Cola or some other brand name in your [twitter_id].

If you're a celebrity and someone has taken over your name you can appeal to Twitter to release the name to you (as mentioned above). When Twitter started a lot of people cybersquatted celebrity names (hoping to sell them to the celebrity at some point, which Twitter wouldn't allow) and even pretended to be the celebrity. Twitter began an authentication process to assure that someone tweeting as a celebrity was actually that celebrity.

Don't Use a Joking or Prank [Twitter_id]

Remember, the name you choose is how people will see you. What seems like a funny joke when you start, might just look really stupid later on and probably limit how successful you'll be on Twitter. Trying to brand stupid across social platforms is, well, stupid.

You are your branding and that's what people will notice. You don't want people thinking you're stupid or childish. Jokes wear thin. A name that seems funny at a bar at 1:00 A.M. might not be such a good idea when you're giving a business presentation and asking people to follow you on Twitter at twitter.com/snuggleface. If you'd feel silly having someone running down the hall trying to catch up with you yelling your [twitter_id], then it's probably not a good [twitter_id].

Stay Away from Racist or Offensive [Twitter_id]'s

Do you really want to be known by a racist epithet? Or by a bodily function, or other things that might be offensive? You're not a little kid. Be adult about what you choose to call yourself on Twitter.

Business Names as a [Twitter_id]

It is ideal for a business to use a variant of their name. If you find someone else is using your company name without your permission you can appeal to Twitter to have the name released to you. If it's recognizable as your company name, or if you have it trademarked, then you shouldn't have any problem getting the name away from the other person.

Don't Use Symbols in Your [Twitter_id]

Forget special symbols (%, $) because they can be confusing and look spammy. Twitter actually rejects many symbols. Also forget about using 3 instead of E, or misspelling words (i.e., @veeagra). Spambots have used these techniques so often they are automatically flagged by Twitter or search engines.

YOUR [TWITTER_ID] IS NOT FIXED IN STONE

Just in case in a moment of frivolity you gave yourself a really stupid [twitter_id] you can change it by changing your [twitter_id] in your profile. You can also change your email address too. What this actually means is that if at some point you want to give your twitterstream to someone else and they want their name on it, it's as simple as changing the name, email address, and other particulars in your Profile. Other social networking sites won't let you do that. For example, there are an extraordinary number of 120+-year-olds on YouTube, the result of people not wanting to give their real birthday and instead erring on the side of phenomenal longevity. Then once they realized how stupid it was, and seeing their age adding an additional year every year, they regretted doing this. But, on YouTube you can't change it. What you signed up with is what you are. On Twitter once you become a bit more mature you can correct the silly things you put on your profile. After all you didn't really win the Nobel Peace Prize, did you?

20

CHAPTER 3

HOW TO SET UP YOUR TWITTER ACCOUNT

TWITTER'S TERMS OF SERVICE (TOS)

Before you create your account you should read Twitter's Terms of Service (TOS). A link to it (Term) is located at the bottom of their home page, or go to twitter.com/tos. It's actually a fairly short TOS. And there's a link at the bottom of the page to an Archive of Previous Terms.

You should also read Twitter's Privacy Policy, linked at the bottom of the page, or go to twitter.com/privacy.

While you're at it you might as well click on the other links at the bottom of the page. The Blog (blog.twitter.com) and Media (media.twitter.com) links are particularly interesting. And the Help link is, well, helpful.

HOW MANY TWITTER ACCOUNTS SHOULD YOU HAVE?

People usually have only one account, and that seems sufficient for most. Twitter doesn't limit you, but you should be reasonable. Here's a good breakdown of accounts if you want to segment your twitterverse:

Personal: About you, but public for others to follow and comment on.

Business: For your business. If you work for someone else they might want you to be the tweeter for the company. In that case this isn't your account. Always keep that in mind. Be very conservative in how you tweet for a company. There are actually terms for tweeting in someone else's name: co-twitterer or ghost twitterer.

This also goes if you are working for a political figure. Many do not actually do some of their own tweeting. So, it is doubly important if you are entrusted to tweet in someone's name that you take the responsibility seriously. Don't even joke about sending jokey tweets. They have a way of accidentally being sent leading to embarrassment for your employer and you probably having to "resign" (be fired).

Hobby: Probably the most fun because you aren't working at it. Hobby tweets shouldn't be stressful. You generally know a lot about your hobby and you bring a certain amount of passion to your tweets. This is a surefire combination for a very successful twitterstream.

Private: A personal twitterstream, but very private, meant for friends and family only. People have to send a request to join, and you have to approve that request in order for them to see your tweets.

Step-by-Step Instructions for Creating Your Twitter Account

Step One: Decide what your [twitter_id] will be. Get an email address with the same user name.

I've given you a lot of suggestions about picking your [twitter_id] (see page 15).

Before creating your account go to live.com (or any other service) and create an email account to match your [twitter_id]. Check to see if it's available first. Easiest way is to just type twitter.com/[twitter_id] (the id you want to use), and see if there's an account for it. If there is the account will come up as active (even though no one seems to be using it, closed, or suspended. Unfortunately, Twitter doesn't release closed or suspended accounts yet. They have said eventually they'll release abandoned accounts (those with just one tweet or have been unused for six months). But, they haven't done so yet.

If no one is using the [twitter_id] and it's available you'll see the following screen:

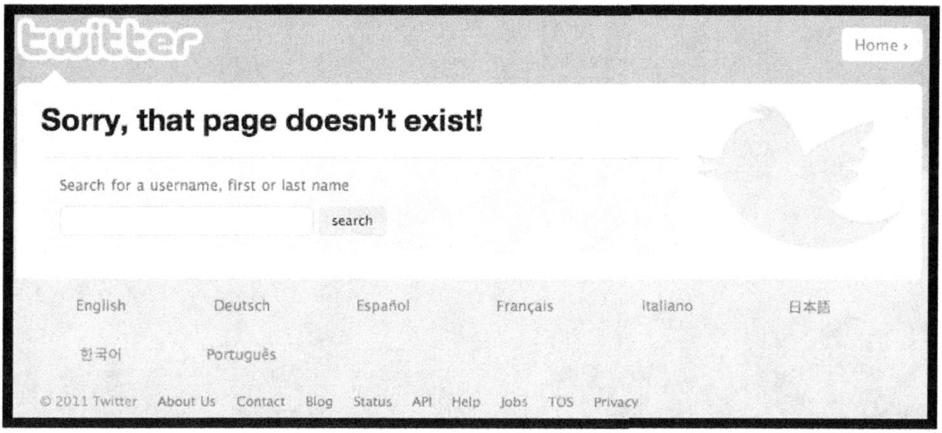

If it doesn't exist, it's available for you.

One reason it's a good idea to have your email address and [twitter_id] the same, is that it's easy to remember. If you have multiple email accounts you might forget which one you're using for which account. You can only use one email per account. You must have a different email for each [twitter_id] you have. If you have lots of accounts that means you have to have lots of email accounts. It's easier to remember when the [twitter_id]'s and email accounts match.

Here's what the blank signup screen looks like.

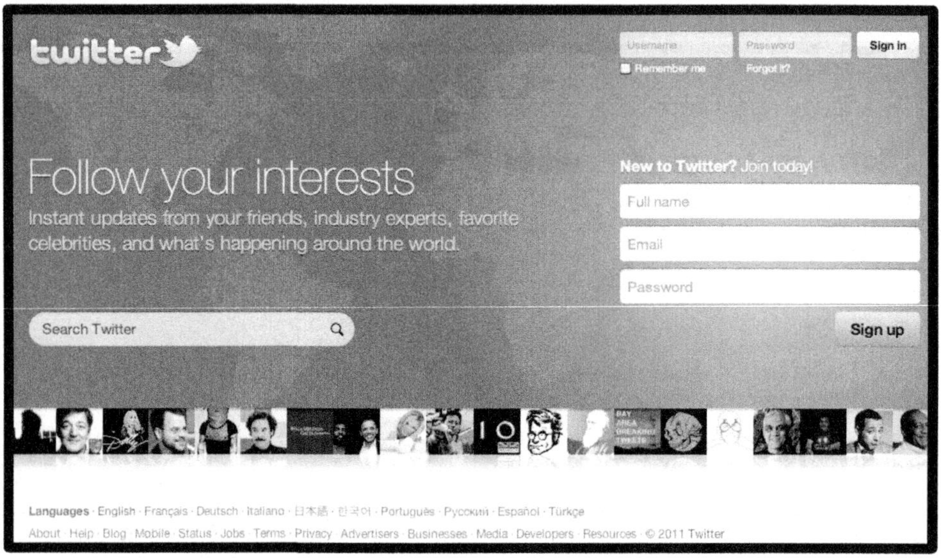

Step Two: Fill in the "New to Twitter? Join today!" Fields.

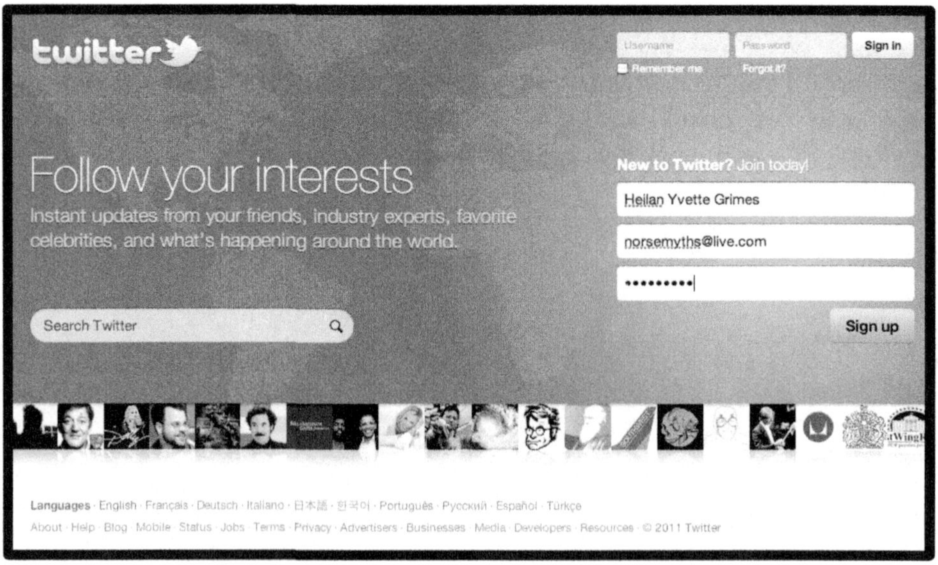

Step Three: Fill out the information fields. Twitter will give you an error message if your name is already in use, if your email is unconfirmed, whether or not your password is okay, and whether or not the [twitter_id] you selected is available.

If your [twitter_id] is already in use they'll give you some, helpful, but usually strange, suggestions. Otherwise keep selecting names until you get one you and Twitter both like.

Then hit "Create my account" to go to the next step.

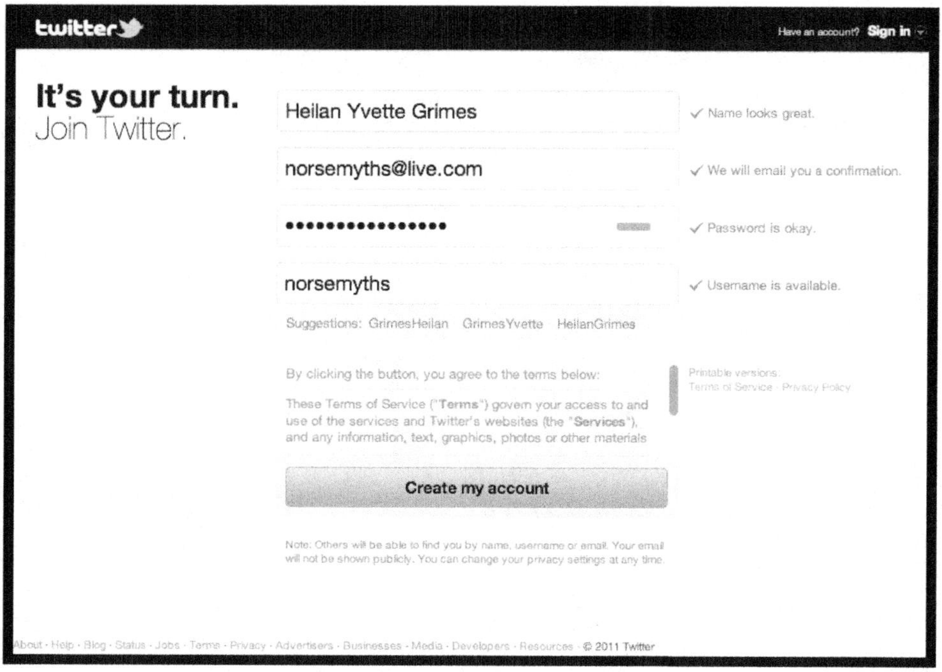

Step Four: Twitter gives you a list of people sorted by interest and friends. You can start following these people immediately or just ignore the suggestions and go to the next section.

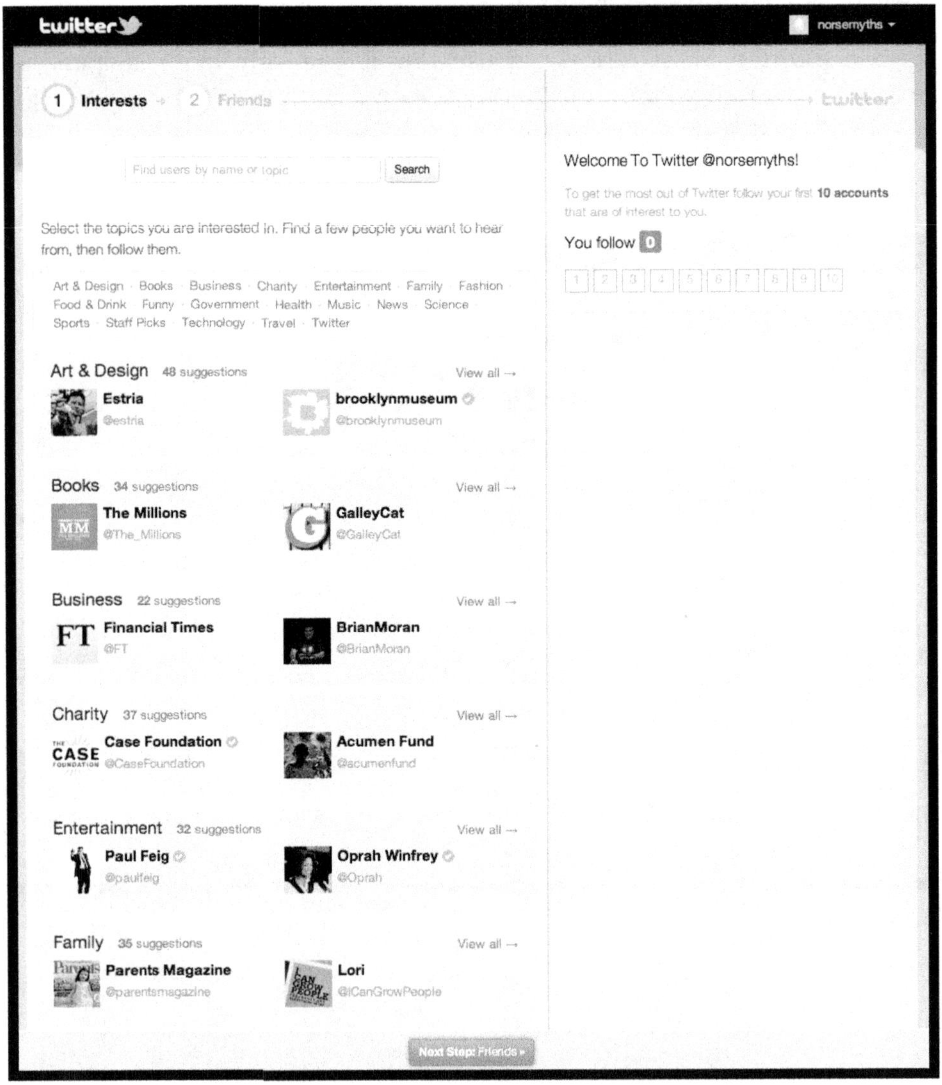

Step Five: You can search for users by name or topic and then follow people from the list that's generated. The next search option on the page gives Twitter permission to look through your contacts (Hotmail, Messenger, Gmail, Yahoo, AOL, LinkedIn) and generate a list of people who also have Twitter accounts. Or, you can choose to skip import.

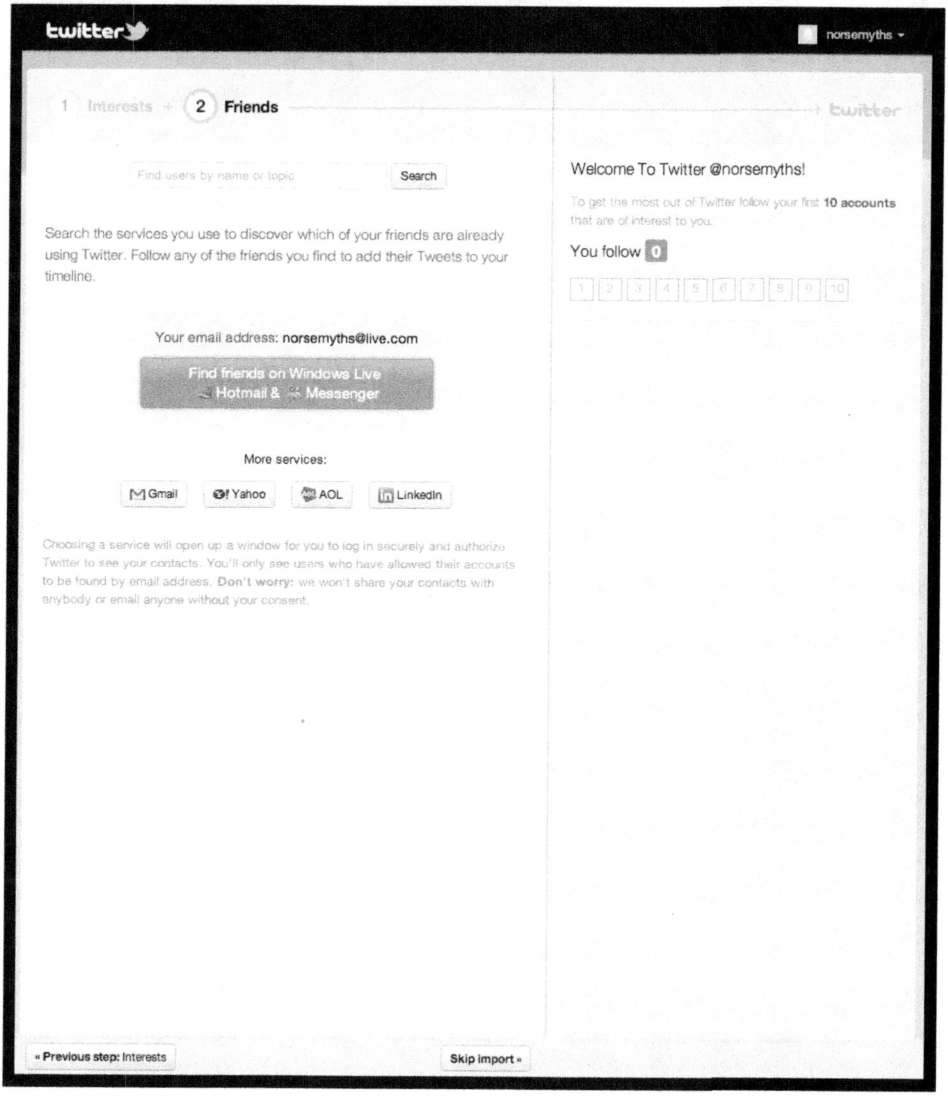

Step Six: This is your home page. It'll look a lot different once you start posting tweets. The left-hand side is your time line where your list of tweets will be. The "What's happening?" box is where you post your tweets.

The right-hand side gives you some further setup options. You can continue looking for twitterers to follow. You can set up mobile notifications on your phone. You can set up your profile, including uploading a profile image and fill out a short bio.

And, finally, you can post your very first tweet. And if you're like lots of people your first tweet will go something like this:

> Hi gang, I'm new and Twitter and just trying to figure out what to post.

The rest of the column includes Trending Topics, and a Twitter suggestion of an app you might find interesting (this suggestion changes all the time).

If you haven't confirmed your email address yet, you'll see the following at the top of this page.

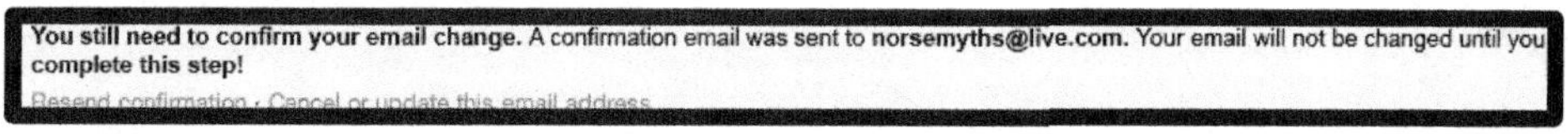

Here's what the confirmation email looks like after you've confirmed it.

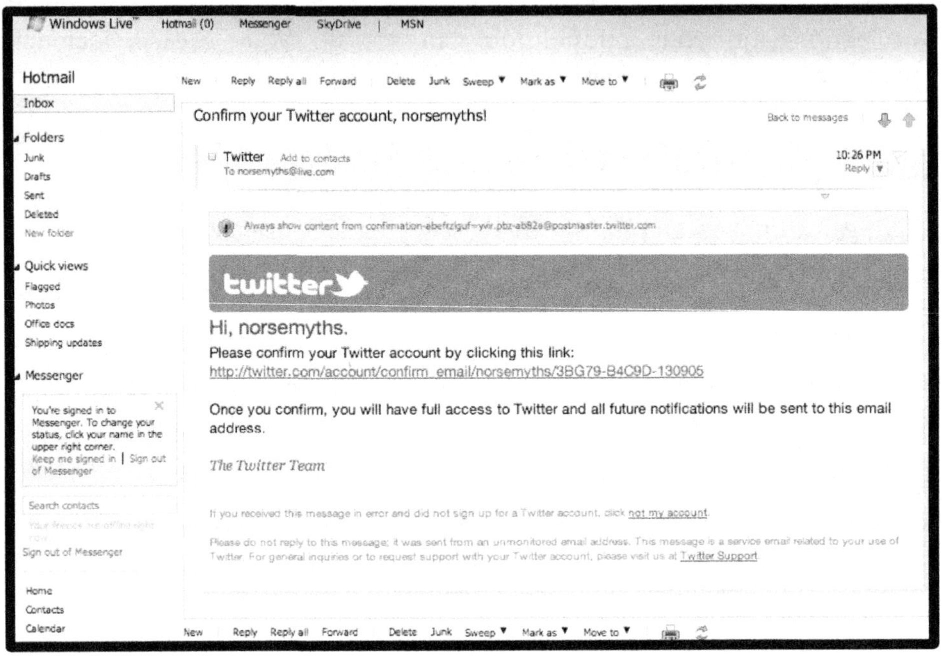

After you've confirmed your email you can go to the next step.

Step Seven: Filling out your account information. Name, Username, Email, Language, TimeZone are pretty standard. I leave the Tweet Location box unchecked. I'm not particularly interested in having people be able to track my location from my tweets. I do check the box Under Tweet Media to show photos and videos from everyone. Otherwise I would only see videos from people I'm following. And when you're starting out that means you'll miss out on just about everything.

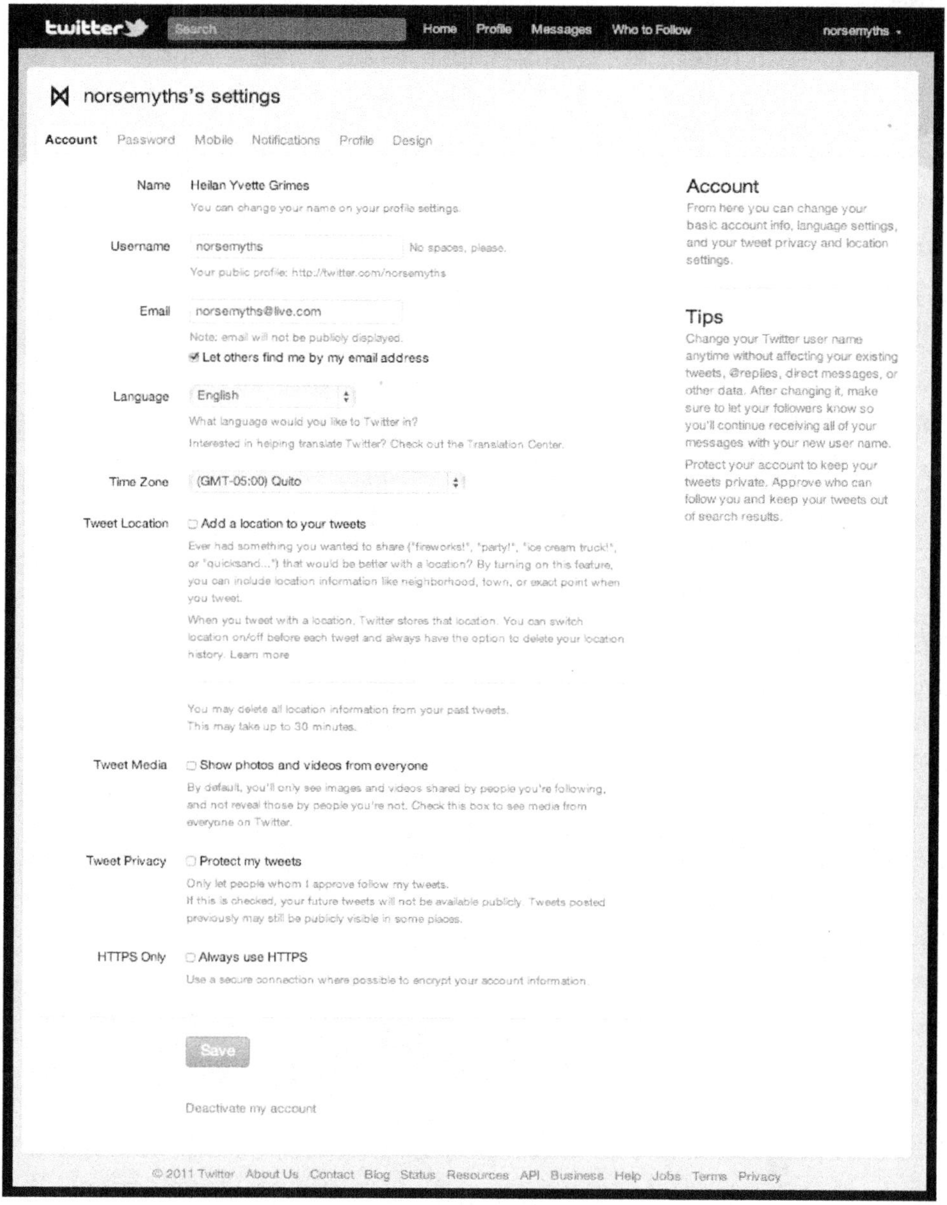
twitter
Search
Home
Profile
Messages
Who to Follow
norsemyths
norsemyths's settings
Account
Password
Mobile
Notifications
Profile
Design
Name
Heilan Yvette Grimes
You can change your name on your profile settings.
Username
norsemyths
No spaces, please.
Your public profile: http://twitter.com/norsemyths
Email
norsemyths@live.com
Note: email will not be publicly displayed.
Let others find me by my email address
Language
English
What language would you like to Twitter in?
Interested in helping translate Twitter? Check out the Translation Center.
Time Zone
(GMT-05:00) Quito
Tweet Location
Add a location to your tweets
Ever had something you wanted to share ("fireworks!", "party!", "ice cream truck!", or "quicksand...") that would be better with a location? By turning on this feature, you can include location information like neighborhood, town, or exact point when you tweet.
When you tweet with a location, Twitter stores that location. You can switch location on/off before each tweet and always have the option to delete your location history. Learn more
You may delete all location information from your past tweets.
This may take up to 30 minutes.
Tweet Media
Show photos and videos from everyone
By default, you'll only see images and videos shared by people you're following, and not reveal those by people you're not. Check this box to see media from everyone on Twitter.
Tweet Privacy
Protect my tweets
Only let people whom I approve follow my tweets.
If this is checked, your future tweets will not be available publicly. Tweets posted previously may still be publicly visible in some places.
HTTPS Only
Always use HTTPS
Use a secure connection where possible to encrypt your account information.
Save
Deactivate my account
Account
From here you can change your basic account info, language settings, and your tweet privacy and location settings.
Tips
Change your Twitter user name anytime without affecting your existing tweets, @replies, direct messages, or other data. After changing it, make sure to let your followers know so you'll continue receiving all of your messages with your new user name.
Protect your account to keep your tweets private. Approve who can follow you and keep your tweets out of search results.
© 2011 Twitter About Us Contact Blog Status Resources API Business Help Jobs Terms Privacy

Don't check "Protect my tweets" if you want followers. If you click the checkbox for Protect my tweets under Tweet Privacy, your tweets will only be visible to those people who send a request to join your twitterstream and whom you approve. Do this only when you want to make everything private and just between you and your followers.

PROTECTED TWEETS

Many people are only on Twitter to communicate with family and friends and don't want others to read their tweets. You have the option of protecting your tweets when you create your Twitter account. This means only people you've approved can see your tweets or respond to them.

If you have protected your tweets then people have to send you a request to follow you. People who protect their tweets rarely give access to strangers. If you want to use Twitter just as a group, fine. But don't expect to get a huge following.

If you haven't protected your tweets and later decide to do so, you can. If you have protected your tweets but decide to hope your twitterstream up to everyone, you can. You are not locked into protected or unprotcted twitterstreams.

If your account is only for friends and family and you aren't interested in everyone in the twitterverse reading your tweets, then check this box. When you do if someone comes to your Twitter account they'll see this (notice the use of one of the default Twitter backgrounds):

Almost 100% of the time a person who has protected their tweets will not accept your request to follow them, so don't bother. These people are not interest in following or being followed except by family and friends. So, if you've sent a request you should cancel it, which you do by going to their [twitter_id] and hitting "Cancel request."

When you're following people and you accidentally follow someone who has protected their tweets (there's a lock next to their [twitter_id] in the list of followers or following), you have sent them a request to join their group. If you don't catch your mistake immediately and unfollow them, you may not notice you've sent them a request. Then while you're doing your Twitter management you might come across that person's "Request sent/Cancel request" screen. You should cancel the request. People who have protected their tweets almost never grant access to a stranger. Cancel request is honored immediately once you hit it. If you refresh the screen you'll see the Send request screen.

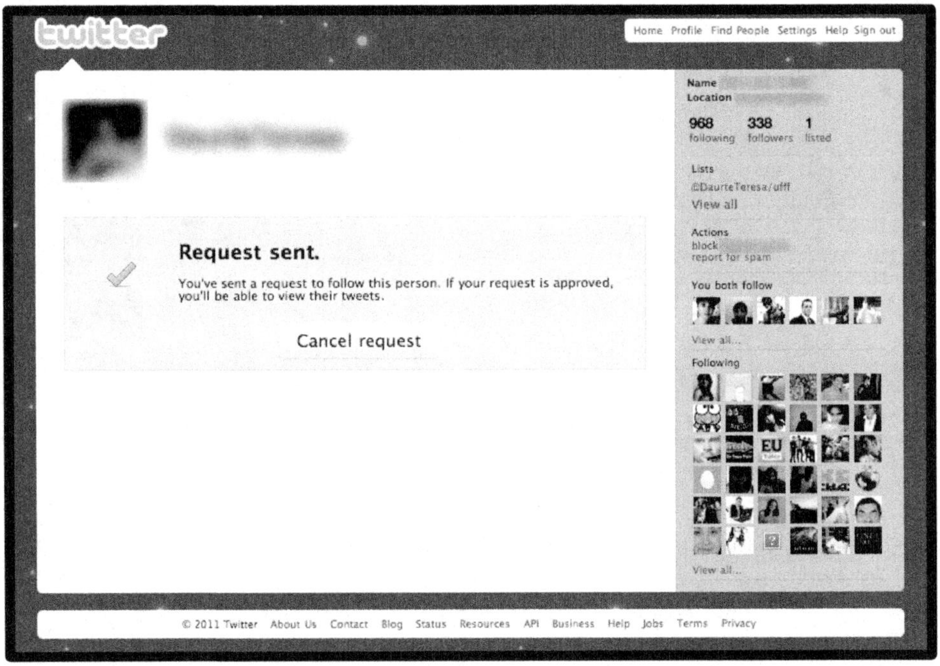

HTTPS Only – Always Use HTTPS

Finally don't check the "HTTPS Only — Always Use HTTPS" on the Account Tab (refer to the account settings on page 31). HTTPS means you're accessing the internet through a secure server. Most times there won't be a secure server connection available, so, you'll find yourself having to override this setting in order to tweet.

That's it for this Tab. Save your settings.

Deactivate My Account

Before moving onto the next Tab notice the "Deactivate my account" link under the Save button. If you ever want to leave Twitter and deactivate your account all you have to do is click on this link and follow the instructions.

After you hit "Deactivate my account" you'll be given an OOPs screen. You can change your mind. If you don't change your mind, once you've deactivated your account all your tweets and followers/following go away. And you cannot reactivate your account without help from Twitter.

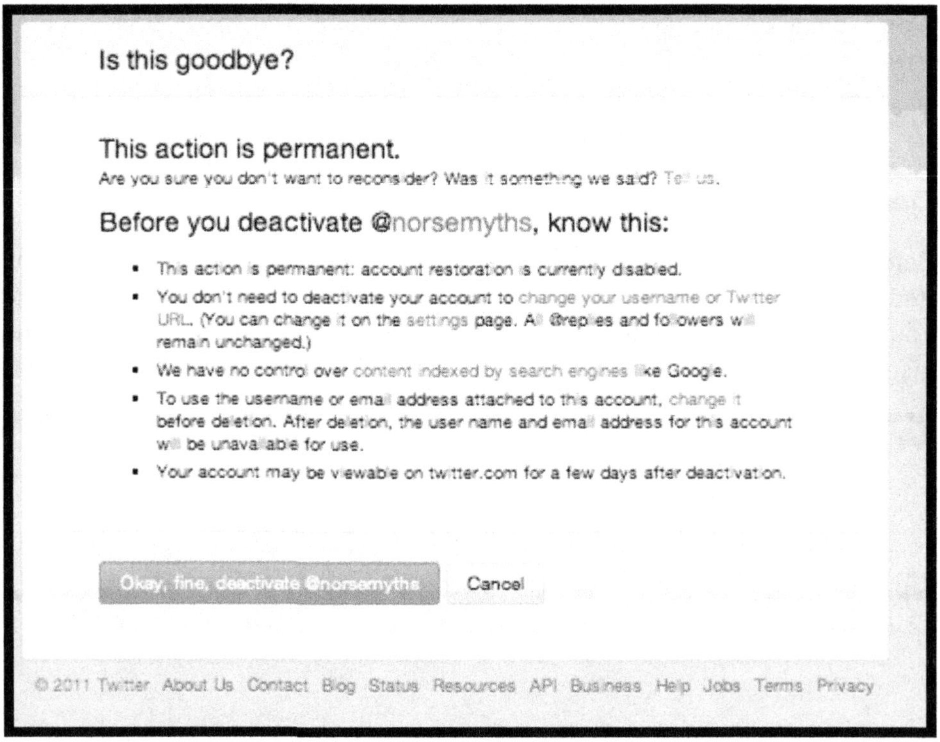

Reactivate My Account (Please, please, pretty please with a cherry on top!)

If you've accidentally deactivated your account, or someone has maliciously signed onto your account and deactivated it for you, there is one way to get it back. You can't reactivate it, but Twitter can. Go to http:support.twitter.com/forms/general and fill out the following form. Twitter has helpfully put in a "With love," closing because they know once they reactivate your account you will be filled with enormous love and gratitude for them. And from then on when you see cute little cuddly kittens, or unicorns in a field of rainbow trees, you'll think of Twitter. You'll name your first child Twitter (Twit for short).

Next to "Reporting" is a dropdown menu. To "Reactivate my account" I chose "Account deactivation/restoration." However there are other menu options you can chose with the "Dear Twitter, please help!" form since it is for more than just reactivating an accidentally deactivated account. If you have any issue you need to contact Twitter about you'll do it from this page. In case your problem isn't one of the pre-defined menu items, the last menu item is all-encompassing: My issue is not in this list! This is unique. Google/YouTube have no option if you don't fall within their pre-defined menu items (shame on your Google/YouTube).

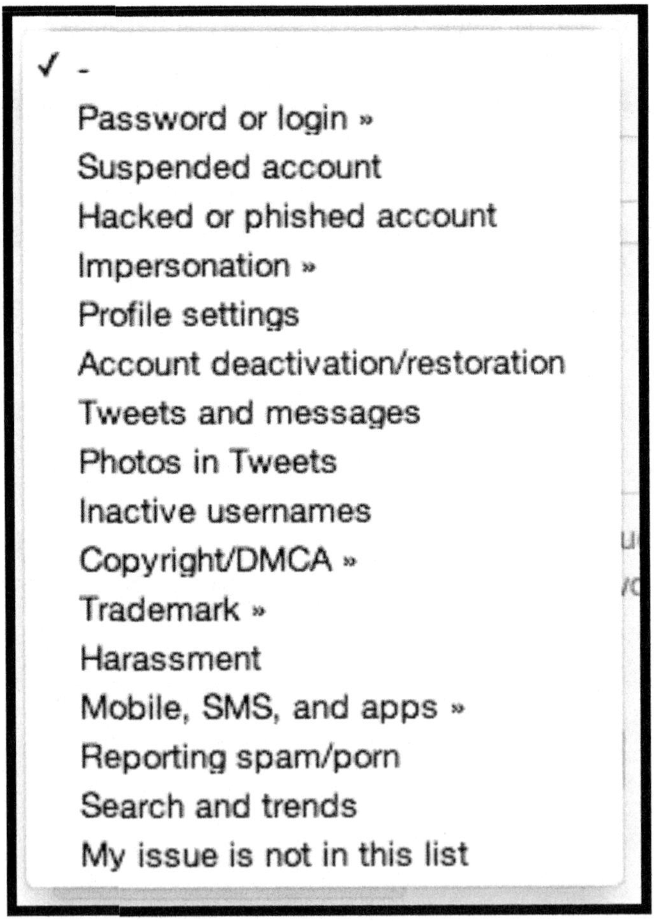

Step Eight: This is the Password Tab where you change your password. Just input your current password, type in a New Password, then type it in again for verification. That's it. Your password has been changed.

I recommend you change your password at least once a month. And don't share it with anyone. Keep all your passwords safe. If you haven't used Google docs, set up a Gmail account and take advantage of Google docs (docs.google.com). You can create a document of all your passwords and keep it online (accessible from any computer) and private.

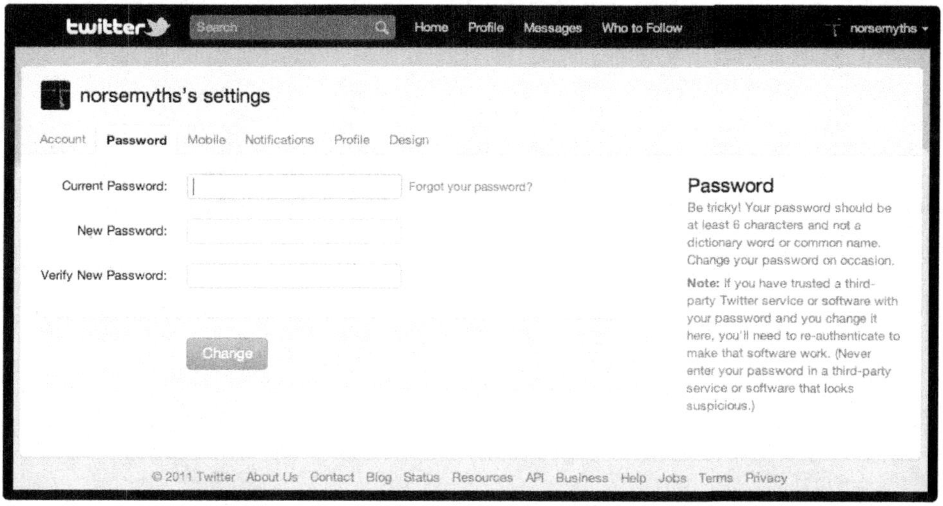

Step Nine: Next is the Mobile Tab that lets you set up Twitter with Text Messaging so you can Send tweets via text messaging from your phone, and Receive texts for DMs as well as tweets from followers. Remember whatever rates you pay for text messaging would apply to any tweets you send or receive via text messaging. The sidebar on the page shows the Twitter commands for using Text Messaging. You can also check out the Mobile Twitter Clients that you can use with your phone (see page 187).

Step Ten: The Notifications Tab is next. This instructs Twitter if or when to send you Messages/Notifications. You can select to either be sent or not sent Email when you receive a DM, a reply to a tweet, or someone mentions you in a tweet. Twitter can also email you when someone follows you, someone marks your tweets as favorites, or when you are retweeted. And finally you can receive a notice when Twitter issues updates or changes, and when there are service updates (usually Twitter is down during service updates). I have all of these checked, but you might not want to receive that many notifications (and I get a lot of notifications). Certainly if you have to pay per text message you'll probably want to turn all these off. You can logon to your computer to get these updates rather than having them sent to your phone. After you've selected your settings hit the Save button and go to the Profile Tab.

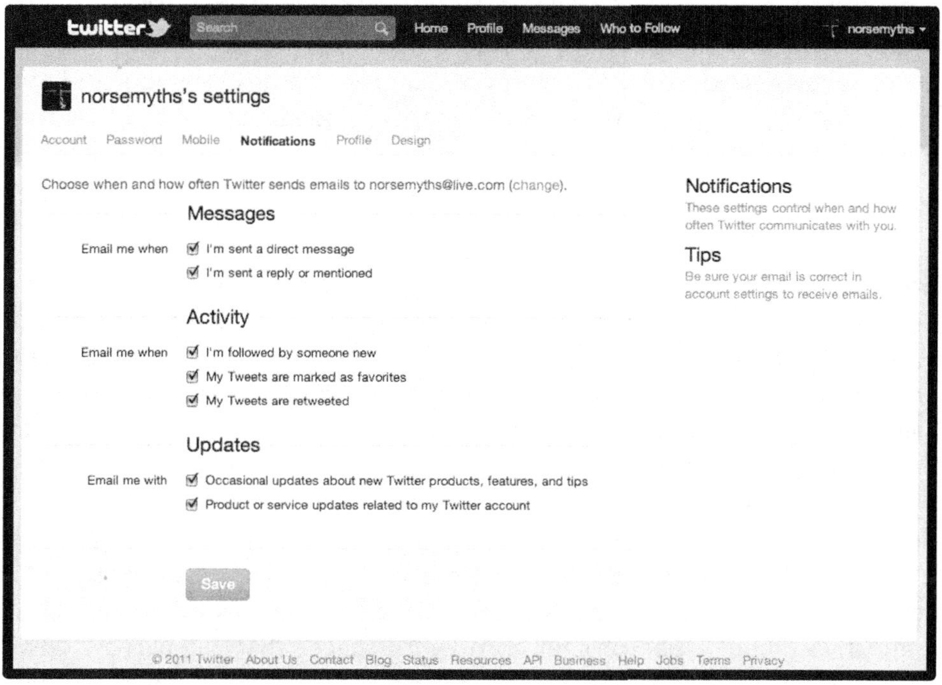

Step Eleven: Next is the Profile Tab. Here you can setup your profile and add an avatar (profile picture). Your profile includes not only what you write in your profile, but also how you present yourself.

Before a lot of people follow someone they first check that person's profile to see who they are so they can eliminate spammers, bots, and automatic programs. They want to make certain you're real, you're you, and you aren't after them for some nefarious reason. It's okay to sell things and let people know you're doing it. It's not okay to try to sell them the Brooklyn Bridge.

Likewise when you follow someone back it might be a good idea to check her/him out (I put her first because the majority of users on Twitter are women, contrary to what teenage boys might think). Do you like their tweets? Do you seem to like the same things? Do you tweet about similar topics? Check their followers to see if you have some in common. The more followers you have in common the more compatible you probably are. If you check someone out and everything seems to be positive, they might be a good person to follow.

The following example shows the Profile Tab with just the name field filled in. Make certain you don't run your name together in the Name field. And don't use underscores to separate your first/middle/last names. So you don't want (using my name as an example) HeilanYvetteGrimes or Heilan_Yvette_Grimes. If someone decides to search for you on Twitter and you've put in your first/middle/last names as one word and they only search for your last name then you won't show up in the search results. Searching for "Grimes" when the Name field says HeilanYvetteGrimes will yield no result. Same thing if you use underscores in-between your first/middle/last names. However searching for "Grimes" when "Heilan Yvette Grimes" (spaces between names) is in the name field will yield a result of every "Grimes" on Twitter who has Grimes listed in the Name Field. If you input a person's full name with spaces that will narrow down your search. So, searching for "Heilan Yvette Grimes" will yield only one result – me. And don't forget to follow me.

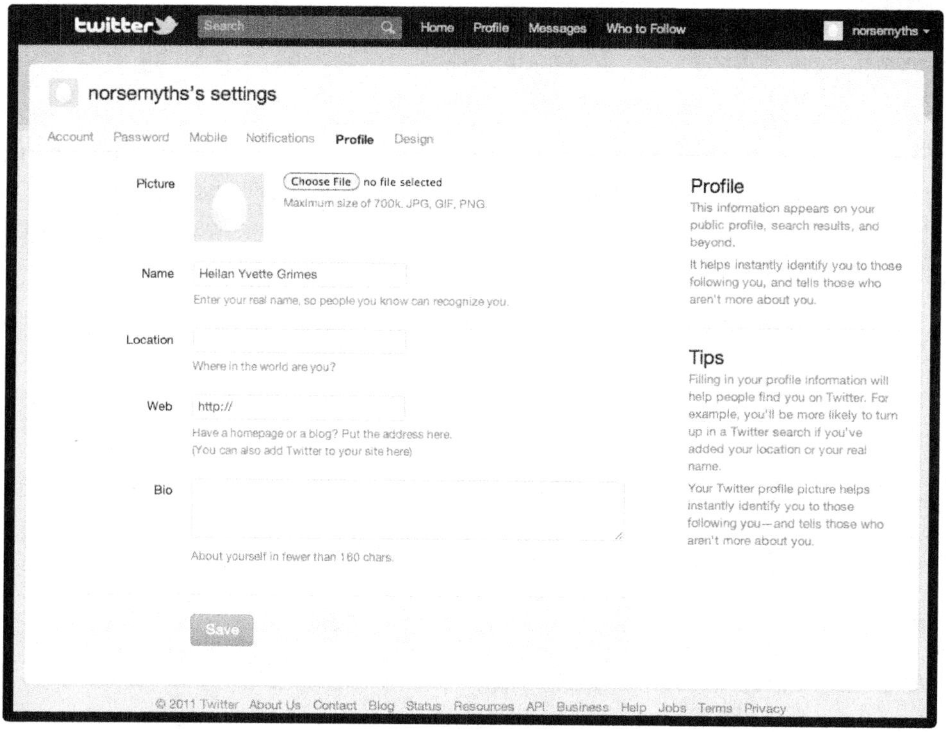

Your Avatar

The first thing you need to do is change the default Twitter profile to an interesting picture. Leaving the default Twitter profile tells people at best you're a newbie and aren't really serious about your Twitter page. At worst it tells people you're a spammer. Spammers typically don't pay much attention to their profile. They put up a Twitter page, do their spamming and are gone in a couple of days, or are taken down by Twitter in a few days once Twitter receives enough complaints. Paying attention to customizing their page isn't a high priority for spammers. So, not having a Profile picture is one indication to others you're a spammer.

However, there are some do's and don'ts to the avatar you choose if you want to be taken seriously.

Remember your avatar is small, so just a headshot if you're going to use your image. Photos even from the waist up can be too small. You want people to see you so they can see what an interesting person you are.

Guys don't post shirtless photos of you posing flexing. People really aren't that interested. They want to see you, and see you as a person not just a flexed torso. And the guys in a lot of those shirtless photos could stand to give up a few beers a night and lose a few pounds.

Gals there's a little more leeway in what you can post. But, if you want to be taken seriously no close-ups of boobs or rear ends even if you are wearing a thong. Photos like that put you in a category you probably don't want to be put in.

DON'T SCARE PEOPLE. People don't follow scary people. Don't put up any picture that makes you look like you're someone carrying a shiv a person might meet in a dark alley. Scary scares people away.

In short be professional, keep your clothes on, don't scare people.

What if you don't want to use your picture as your avatar? That's okay. I don't use my picture as my avatar. Put up something interesting. You just want to avoid the default Profile image.

NO CUTE KITTENS! Okay, I've thought about it. Only really really cute fluffy kittens. And only if home and fun is the purpose of your account. Unless, of course, you're selling cute kittens. If you want to use animal pictures for business, be more professional. Though an element of fun is okay.

Cartoon images don't really work that well unless you're a cartoonist and it's your work. People want to follow real people. And many cartoon characters are copyrighted.

The photo you put up reflects you. If you want to be taken as someone who is professional and serious, then put up a serious photo. If you're silly (or a comedian) put up a silly one. But don't complain if people find you silly.

The best test is to look at the avatar you're going to post. Would you follow someone with an avatar like that?

All of the above being said, there are always exceptions to what I've written. Just use good judgment.

The original default Twitter avatar was the o_O ideogram. It means surprise or disbelief. Maybe the founders were surprised at how many people wanted to send 140-character messages?

Now Twitter uses eggs because of Twitter being birdlike, and birds start as eggs and you're just starting your life on Twitter, so the default egg represents your start. They come in many colors. If you are viewing this file as a PDF you'll see colors. If you're viewing it in print, or on a B&W electronic reader, then you'll only see shades of gray. Here are the basic colors. If you have any other colors please send them to me.

Here are the alternate default Twitterbirds profiles. If you know of any other colors let me know.

Profile Sizes and Resolutions

You should replace the default bird's egg/twitterbird image with your own profile picture. It should be square if you want to fill the entire box. The profile box with a minimum resolution of 72 ppi (pixels per inch) is 149x149 points (2.069" x 2.069"). However, you can import larger sizes, which Twitter will scale down to fit the default size, but without losing resolution. I recommend this because it will give you a better profile picture.

If you click on a profile picture it will take you to a screen with the image in it's upload size. I've found that a square of 96x96 points with a resolution of 300 ppi works very nicely. It gives you a file size of about 440k. Twitter will not upload a profile picture larger than 700k. So if you want higher resolution or size you still have some leeway. Twitter accepts gifs, jpgs, or pngs. The profile field is square. So if you upload a horizontal or vertical rectangle it will not fill the entire area. Of course, if you load an extremely large non-square image it will be cropped and probably not display as you would like.

Other Information

Name, Location, Web, and Bio information appears in the upper right of your Twitter profile page.

Don't put in specific address information. You don't have to just because they ask for it. Think about it? Do you really want your home address broadcast to everyone on the Internet? The Internet is not always a warm and fuzzy place.

Don't leave the field blank. People are more likely to follow you if you aren't a stranger. Leave at the most a city and state. Most people just put in their state or area of the country (New England, Midwest, etc.). If you are a business you can be a little more specific.

The Web link will appear as a hotlink in your profile so that anyone clicking on it will be taken to wherever the link redirects, i.e., to your website.

It's very important to fill in some biographical information. More people will follow you if you do, since having biographical information shows that you're a real person (or at least play a real person on the internet). Tell them why you're on twitter, what you plan to do, how you can help them. And do it in 160 characters or less, only 20 characters larger than a tweet. That's not a whole lot of space for so much information. However in the Background Design section I'll give you some helpful hints on how to get around that (see page 51).

There's another reason it's important to fill in this information. Your Profile information and your tweets are what Google searches and indexes. If you're a company and want Google to find your twitterstream this area has to be filled in with some information.

Common Mistakes

CHECK YOUR SPELLING! You'll lose credibility if you have spelling mistakes in your Profile.

- Your (belonging to you), not you're (abbreviation for you are)
- Its (possessive form of it, belonging to it), not it's (abbreviation for it is)

Here's a filled out Profile Tab.

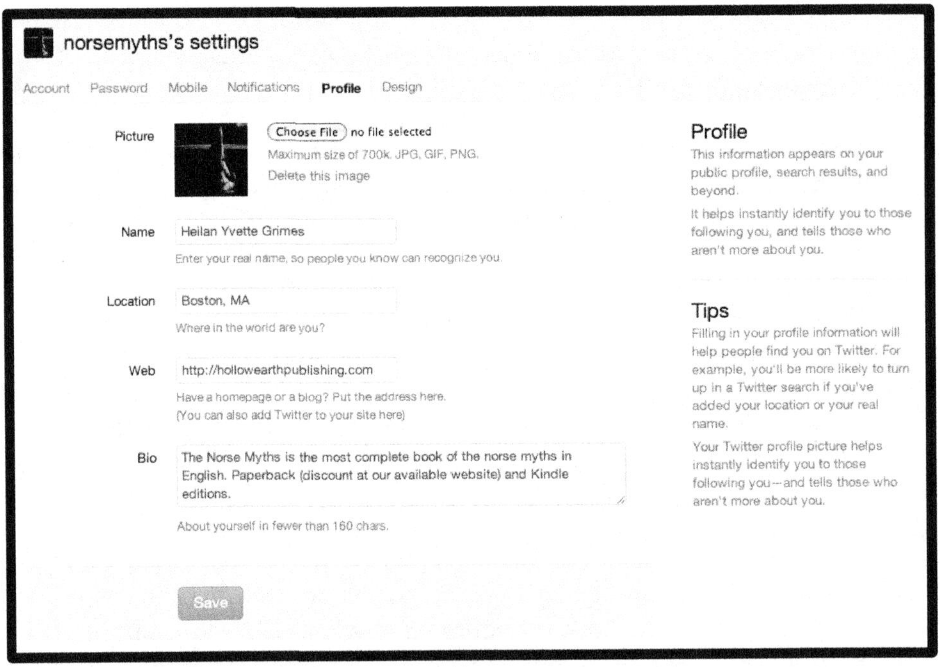

Once you are satisfied with your entries, Save and click on the Design Tab.

Step Twelve: The Design Tab gives you the ability to make your Twitter page uniquely your own,

You can add a background to your entire page, change font colors, and change the background for sections on your page.

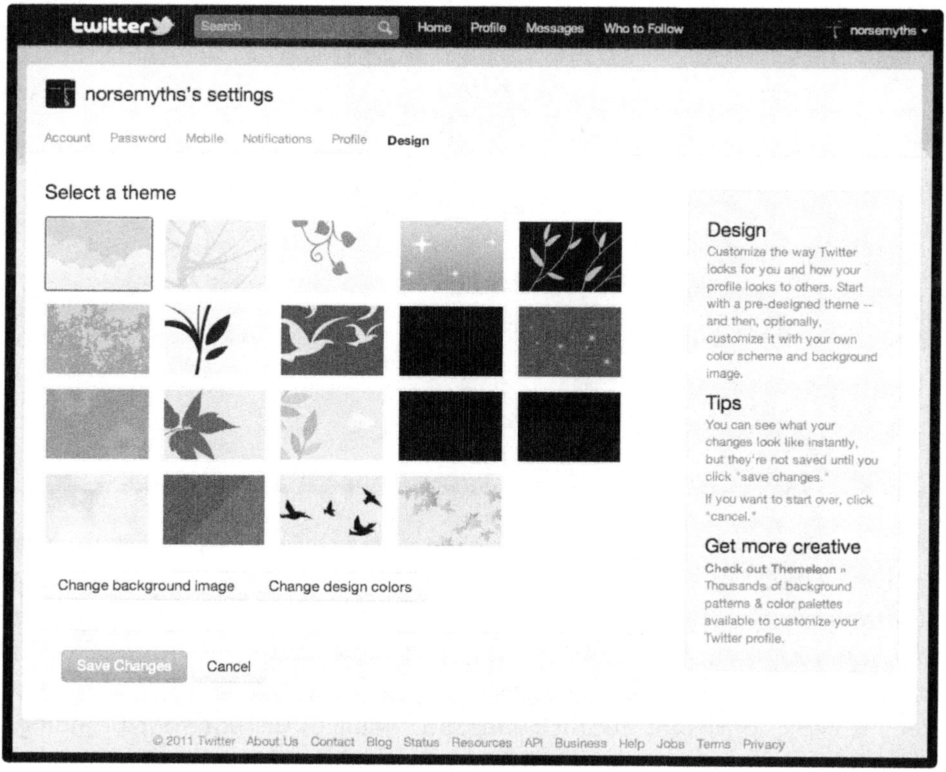

You have the option of changing the background image as well as changing the design colors.

Here's the norsemyths Twitter channel with the yellow default background (if you're viewing this in a printed book, or on a B&W reader, then use your imagination, it looks pretty garish):

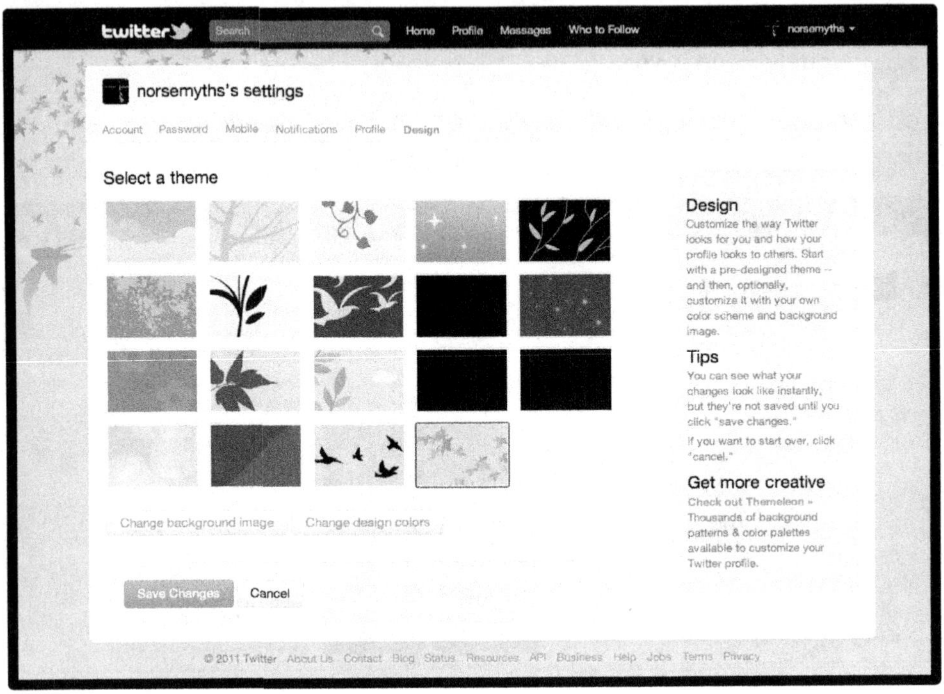

After you've made your selections click on Save Changes and your basic Twitter setup is done. Now go to your Home page (twitter.com/[twitter_id] to see what it looks like. You can always make changes anytime you want. And you probably will since you'll get tired of seeing the same old thing. Though, if you've branded your site you might want to keep it fairly consistent because you don't want to disrupt your branding.

Some nice settings for the "Change design colors" button:

- background: Theme 9
- text 000000
- links 082680
- sidebar d6d6d6
- sidebar border 000000
- The Center and Sidebar Sections

You also have some design options for the center tweets section. Next to the "Change background image" button is the "Change design colors" button. Click on it and you'll see several options. You can change the background color of the center section, change the text color, change the links color, change the sidebar background color, and change the sidebar border.

True you can use a pink background in the center section and green type for your tweets. But no one is going to be able to read them. Remember a lot of people actually are colorblind. Keep the center section simple. Leave the background white and the text black. Anything other than that and reading comprehension plummets. Same rules for the sidebar. Make it complementary to your background image. But, don't make it unreadable. Reading comprehension with white text on a dark or black background. So don't get cutesy and use a black background with white type. Red/blue and blue/red make your eyes dance around. Just be careful what colors you choose for the sidebar.

CREATING A SPECIALIZED BACKGROUND

I already discussed the basics of your Twitter Profile (see page 42). The information you can post to your profile is very limited, skimpy in fact. You won't be able to tell everyone about your multiple websites or social network contacts. But, there is a solution.

You can create a branded background with all that information on it. You can include lots of contact information. If you want you can include Telephone/Fax/Cell numbers, addresses, facebook, twitter, LinkedIn, Foursquare, whatever other social networks you belong to. You can list websites, links to portfolios, flickr, etc. Instead of people looking at the usually cutoff information in the top right, they can look at extensive information on the left sidebar of your Twitter page.

Here's where you can post an extended biography. Your bio is important. Don't be shy. If you're an expert in something, say so. Your bio should push what you want to do on Twitter. If you have a book to sell mention it in the sidebar. Post a cover image of your book with a link to an order page.

Although you can list websites, you can't put in hotlinks to them. So, make certain you include the URL: TheBookofTwitter.com for example. You don't need the http:// or www anymore since browsers automatically put that in.

About Background Images

Background images are fixed from the left side. They don't resize. If someone views your background image on a monitor larger than your background image, then your background image will tile (repeat itself).

You're background image shouldn't be overly complicated. You don't want to take away from the center section where your tweets are. Your background image should be there, present you nicely, but not distract people.

Don't go on and on and on and on and on in your sidebar with lots of references, busy graphics, etc. Short, sweet, and interesting. Make others want to follow you. Make the information specific enough so people know exactly why you're on Twitter. If you're promoting your business on Twitter, leave no doubt what kind of business it is. Don't be obtuse. If most of your tweets are going to be about vacuum cleaners, then make certain they know that from the information in your sidebar.

All of your address references, website references, company references, addresses, etc. have to be incorporated in your background image. There are no hotlinks. People will have to type the URL in their browser. If you have a long, complicated URL, use a link shortener. I use goo.gl because if I'm signed into my Gmail account, Google will track how many people use that link. Otherwise you'll wonder if anyone clicked on it at all.

Rules for Designing an Informational Background Image

- Only put information on the left-hand side of your Twitter background because of how the window resizes when a website page is viewed on different-sized monitors.
- Make the design interesting but not intrusive. Blocks work. Post-it® note images going down the left-hand side with information on each Post-it® works. Making your background a bulletin board with the Post-its® on the left-hand side works.
- Generally black type on a very light background (I prefer gray, but any light color) is more legible.
- Twitter background sizes in pixels. Save as a jpeg or png. The lower sizes will give you a larger image.
  - 1024 x 768
  - 1280 x 1024
  - 1440 x 900
  - 1600 x 1200
  - 1680 x 1050
  - 1920 x 1200
- **fuelyourcreativity.com/free-psd-twitter-background-template** Free PhotoShop Twitter Background Template compliments of Chad Engle (Thank you Chad)
- If you aren't using an image, a gradient is an easy alternative and works better than solid backgrounds

BACKGROUND CREATORS

There are people who charge nominal fees to design Twitter backgrounds. Just Google "twitter backgrounds" and you'll find a lot of free ones, too. The following are some sources I came up with.

A lot of these Twitter background sites give you downloadable images to use in your design. Most assume you're going to be working in PhotoShop. But PhotoShop is a very expensive program, and not a lot of people use it. If you have Adobe's Photo Elements you can use these downloads. And they work with lots of other imaging programs. However there is the magnificent Gimp.

Gimp

gimp.org

If you don't have an imaging program you are not out of luck. There's a free program (Mac and PC compatible) you can download. Since it was developed for the NIH (National Institute of Health) with taxpayer dollars the program is free to download and use. It is very close to Adobe Photoshop. It can use PhotoShop plug-ins and can open PhotoShop files in layers if that file was created in layers. The program is called Gimp and you can download your free copy at gimp.org. There's extensive documentation on the site as well as tutorials. There are links to books you can purchase.

Free Twitter Designer

freetwitterdesigner.com

Incredibly easy, full-featured, free Twitter background creator. If you know nothing about design, use this and you'll be amazed at the results.

Tweetstyle

tweetstyle.com

Free Twitter backgrounds and they can even make one for you.

My Tweetspace

mytweetspace.com

Free Twitter backgrounds

Custom Backgrounds for Twitter

custombackgroundsfortwitter.com/gallery/category/custom

Free if you add a link and have 3000+ followers, otherwise $100

Twitbacks

twitbacks.com/create-twitbacks-account.php

Free backgrounds

The Closet Entrepreneur

theclosetentrepreneur.com

Create a Twitter background using PowerPoint or Keynote.

Stripe Generator

stripegenerator.com

Use this background generator to make a stripey background.

Twitip

twitip.com

Seven free backgrounds to download and customize. These are particularly nice. You can open them in PhotoShop. They already have the text layers prepared for you to customize.

Free Twitter Designer

freetwitterdesigner.com

Free online background designer that can sign into your account by OAuth and automatically upload the background you design.

Pelfusion

pelfusion.com/freebies/free-twitter-background-templates-with-psd-files/

Free background PhotoShop files. Look at the other parts of their site, too. Great graphics website.

Finally, the Applications Tab

You can reach the Applications Tab by using the menu bar:

Settings > Applications

or you can use this URL twitter.com/account/connections.

When you go to some websites they ask you to let them sign in to your website using OAuth identification. Any websites you've given permission to access your Twitter account is listed here. And this is where you can rescind that permission by just clicking on the Revoke Access button.

The OAuth identification is a vast improvement over how Twitter originally did it, which was no official access at all. If you wanted to subscribe to the Twitter services a website offered you had to give them access to your Twitter page by actually giving them your Twitter login and password. Which meant they could log onto your Twitter page and have 100% access to do anything they wanted. The only way to stop their access was to go in and change your password login. Of course, some people would find the service they'd subscribed too wasn't on the up and up and had changed their password, and in some instances even the name and email for their Twitter account. Twitter usually would give access back to the original owner and block the service.

Of course a lot of spammers would lure people in with some legitimate useful Twitter features, and once they had access to a person's Twitter account would proceed to spam other accounts using the login/password access they had.

This was a terrible situation and Twitter started using OAuth authentication which let twitterers give a website limited access to their Twitter account. Enough for them to do whatever services they were offering. And it was easy to rescind that permission.

If you come across a website asking for your login and password, don't give it. This means that website has either not applied for OAuth access or has applied and been denied. Either way it should raise your suspicions and lots of red flags. There is absolutely no reason for a website to ask for your actual login and password. Do not give it out.

The following are screenshots of just some of my OAuth authorizations. The reason there are so many is that I am constantly testing Twitter applications to see which are the best, and unfortunately which are the worst. So, don't take any of these applications as being endorsed by me. They might be, but it might be that I am only testing for a day and then will revoke access.

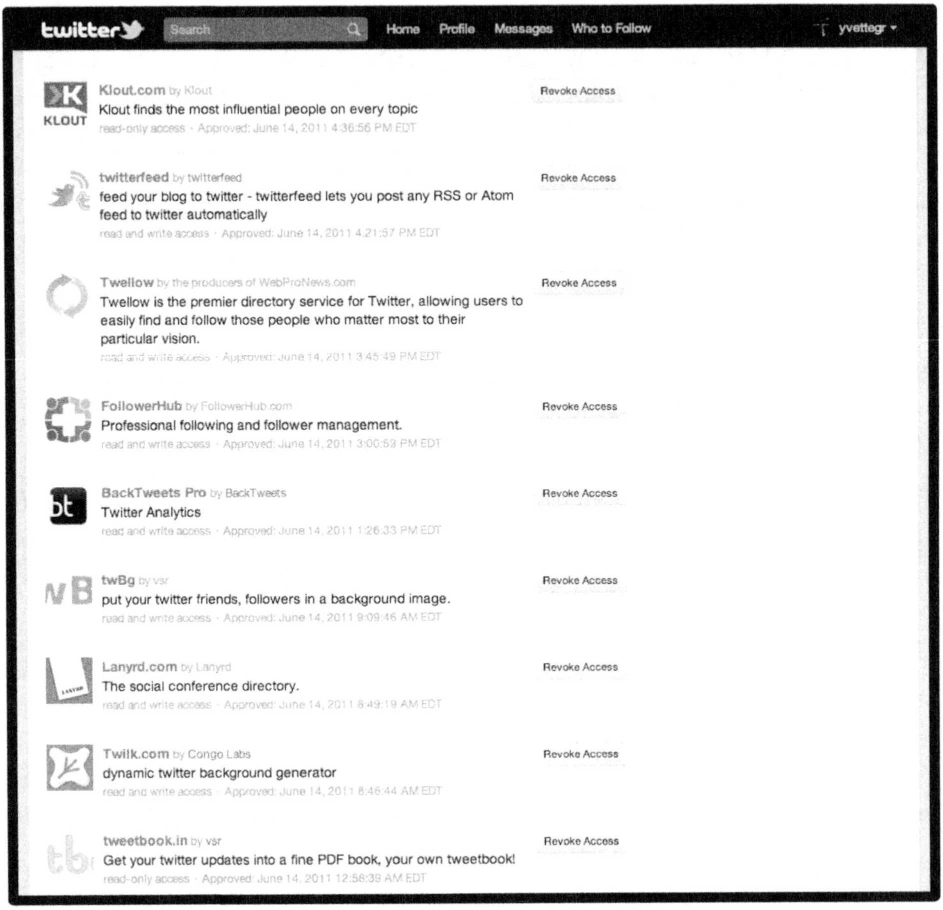
twitter
Search
Home
Profile
Messages
Who to Follow
yvettegr
Klout.com by Klout
Klout finds the most influential people on every topic
read-only access · Approved: June 14, 2011 4:36:56 PM EDT
Revoke Access
twitterfeed by twitterfeed
feed your blog to twitter - twitterfeed lets you post any RSS or Atom feed to twitter automatically
read and write access · Approved: June 14, 2011 4:21:57 PM EDT
Revoke Access
Twellow by the producers of WebProNews.com
Twellow is the premier directory service for Twitter, allowing users to easily find and follow those people who matter most to their particular vision.
read and write access · Approved: June 14, 2011 3:45:49 PM EDT
Revoke Access
FollowerHub by FollowerHub.com
Professional following and follower management.
read and write access · Approved: June 14, 2011 3:00:53 PM EDT
Revoke Access
BackTweets Pro by BackTweets
Twitter Analytics
read and write access · Approved: June 14, 2011 1:26:33 PM EDT
Revoke Access
twBg by vsr
put your twitter friends, followers in a background image.
read and write access · Approved: June 14, 2011 9:09:46 AM EDT
Revoke Access
Lanyrd.com by Lanyrd
The social conference directory.
read and write access · Approved: June 14, 2011 8:49:19 AM EDT
Revoke Access
Twilk.com by Congo Labs
dynamic twitter background generator
read and write access · Approved: June 14, 2011 8:46:44 AM EDT
Revoke Access
tweetbook.in by vsr
Get your twitter updates into a fine PDF book, your own tweetbook!
read-only access · Approved: June 14, 2011 12:58:39 AM EDT
Revoke Access

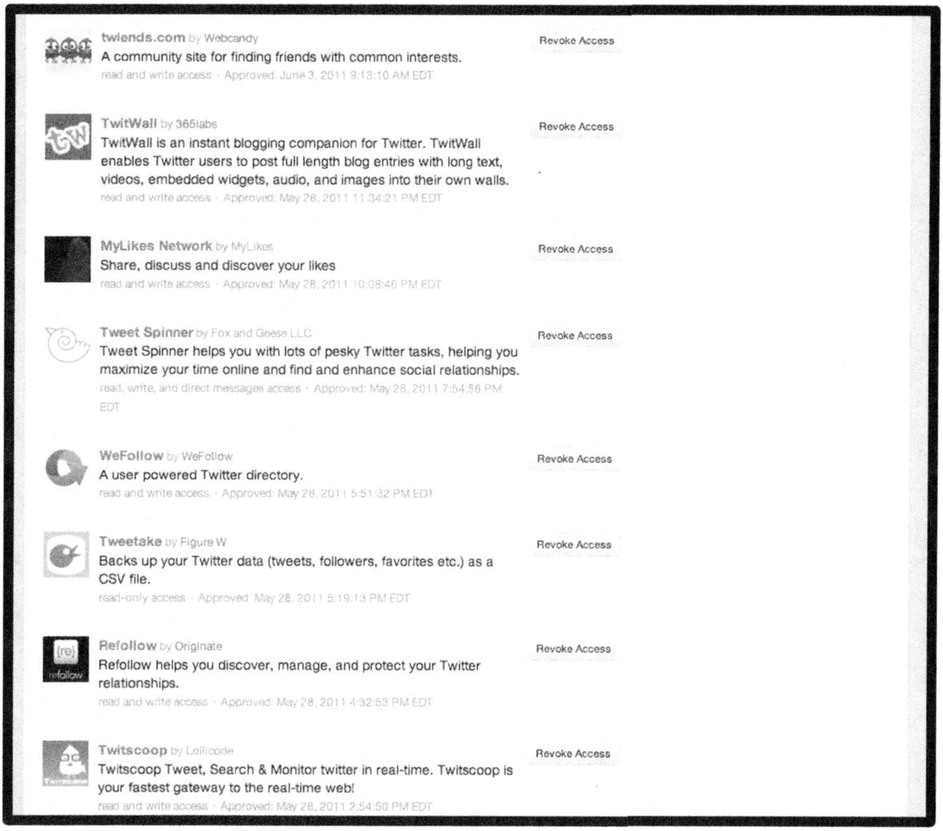
twiends.com by Webcandy
A community site for finding friends with common interests.
read and write access · Approved: June 3, 2011 9:13:10 AM EDT
Revoke Access
TwitWall by 365labs
TwitWall is an instant blogging companion for Twitter. TwitWall enables Twitter users to post full length blog entries with long text, videos, embedded widgets, audio, and images into their own walls.
read and write access · Approved: May 28, 2011 11:34:21 PM EDT
Revoke Access
MyLikes Network by MyLikes
Share, discuss and discover your likes
read and write access · Approved: May 28, 2011 10:08:46 PM EDT
Revoke Access
Tweet Spinner by Fox and Geese LLC
Tweet Spinner helps you with lots of pesky Twitter tasks, helping you maximize your time online and find and enhance social relationships.
read, write, and direct messages access · Approved: May 28, 2011 7:54:58 PM EDT
Revoke Access
WeFollow by WeFollow
A user powered Twitter directory.
read and write access · Approved: May 28, 2011 5:51:32 PM EDT
Revoke Access
Tweetake by Figure W
Backs up your Twitter data (tweets, followers, favorites etc.) as a CSV file.
read-only access · Approved: May 28, 2011 5:19:13 PM EDT
Revoke Access
Refollow by Originate
Refollow helps you discover, manage, and protect your Twitter relationships.
read and write access · Approved: May 28, 2011 4:32:53 PM EDT
Revoke Access
Twitscoop by Lollicode
Twitscoop Tweet, Search & Monitor twitter in real-time. Twitscoop is your fastest gateway to the real-time web!
read and write access · Approved: May 28, 2011 2:54:50 PM EDT
Revoke Access

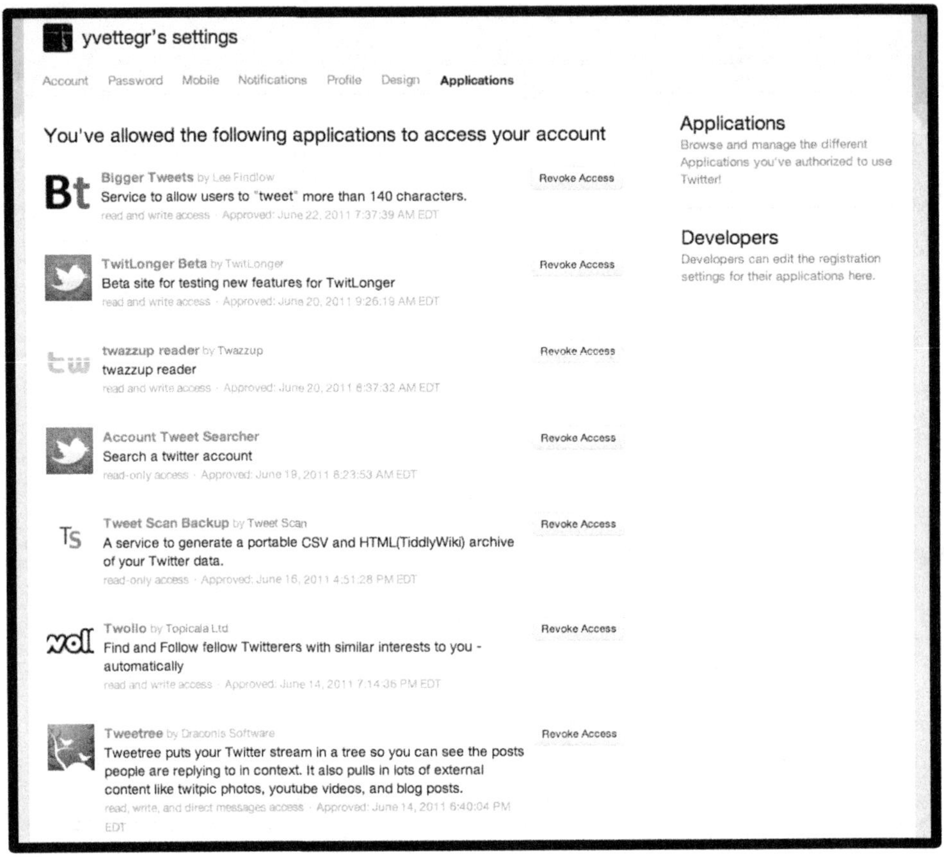
yvettegr's settings
Account Password Mobile Notifications Profile Design Applications
You've allowed the following applications to access your account
Bigger Tweets by Lee Findlow
Service to allow users to "tweet" more than 140 characters.
read and write access · Approved: June 22, 2011 7:37:39 AM EDT
Revoke Access
TwitLonger Beta by TwitLonger
Beta site for testing new features for TwitLonger
read and write access · Approved: June 20, 2011 9:26:19 AM EDT
Revoke Access
twazzup reader by Twazzup
twazzup reader
read and write access · Approved: June 20, 2011 8:37:32 AM EDT
Revoke Access
Account Tweet Searcher
Search a twitter account
read-only access · Approved: June 19, 2011 8:23:53 AM EDT
Revoke Access
Tweet Scan Backup by Tweet Scan
A service to generate a portable CSV and HTML(TiddlyWiki) archive of your Twitter data.
read-only access · Approved: June 16, 2011 4:51:28 PM EDT
Revoke Access
Twollo by Topicala Ltd
Find and Follow fellow Twitterers with similar interests to you - automatically
read and write access · Approved: June 14, 2011 7:14:36 PM EDT
Revoke Access
Tweetree by Draconis Software
Tweetree puts your Twitter stream in a tree so you can see the posts people are replying to in context. It also pulls in lots of external content like twitpic photos, youtube videos, and blog posts.
read, write, and direct messages access · Approved: June 14, 2011 6:40:04 PM EDT
Revoke Access
Applications
Browse and manage the different Applications you've authorized to use Twitter!
Developers
Developers can edit the registration settings for their applications here.

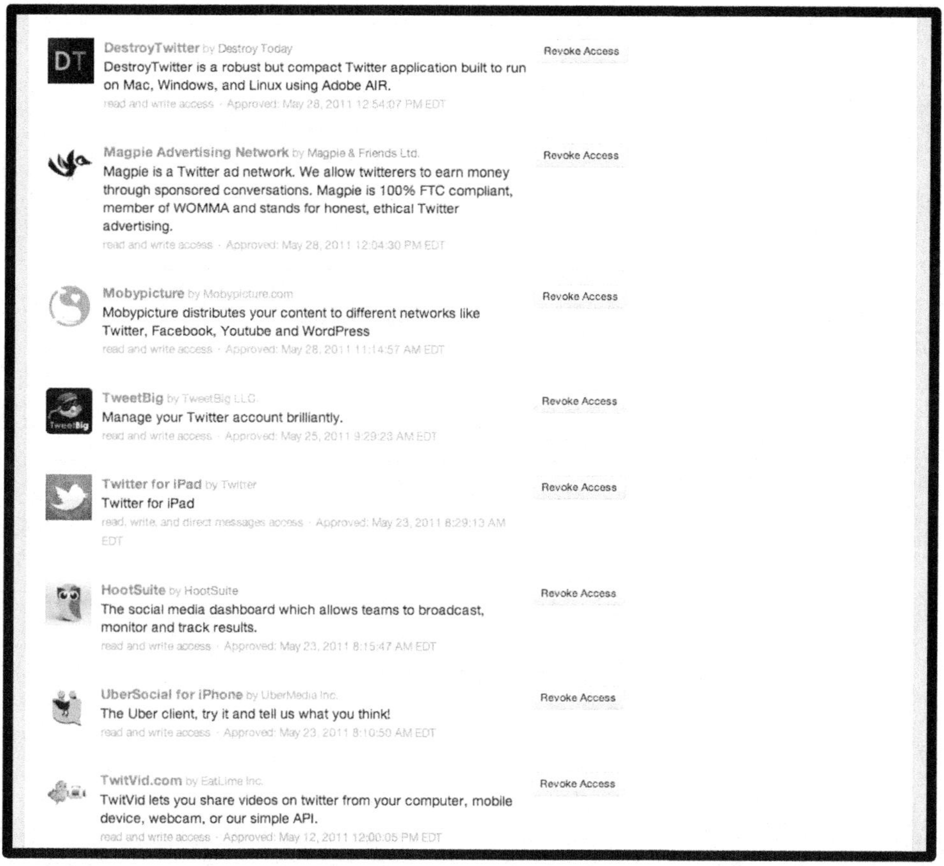
DestroyTwitter by Destroy Today
DestroyTwitter is a robust but compact Twitter application built to run on Mac, Windows, and Linux using Adobe AIR.
read and write access · Approved: May 28, 2011 12:54:07 PM EDT
Revoke Access
Magpie Advertising Network by Magpie & Friends Ltd.
Magpie is a Twitter ad network. We allow twitterers to earn money through sponsored conversations. Magpie is 100% FTC compliant, member of WOMMA and stands for honest, ethical Twitter advertising.
read and write access · Approved: May 28, 2011 12:04:30 PM EDT
Revoke Access
Mobypicture by Mobypicture.com
Mobypicture distributes your content to different networks like Twitter, Facebook, Youtube and WordPress
read and write access · Approved: May 28, 2011 11:14:57 AM EDT
Revoke Access
TweetBig by TweetBig LLC
Manage your Twitter account brilliantly.
read and write access · Approved: May 25, 2011 9:29:23 AM EDT
Revoke Access
Twitter for iPad by Twitter
Twitter for iPad
read, write, and direct messages access · Approved: May 23, 2011 8:29:13 AM EDT
Revoke Access
HootSuite by HootSuite
The social media dashboard which allows teams to broadcast, monitor and track results.
read and write access · Approved: May 23, 2011 8:15:47 AM EDT
Revoke Access
UberSocial for iPhone by UberMedia Inc.
The Uber client, try it and tell us what you think!
read and write access · Approved: May 23, 2011 8:10:50 AM EDT
Revoke Access
TwitVid.com by EatLime Inc.
TwitVid lets you share videos on twitter from your computer, mobile device, webcam, or our simple API.
read and write access · Approved: May 12, 2011 12:00:05 PM EDT
Revoke Access

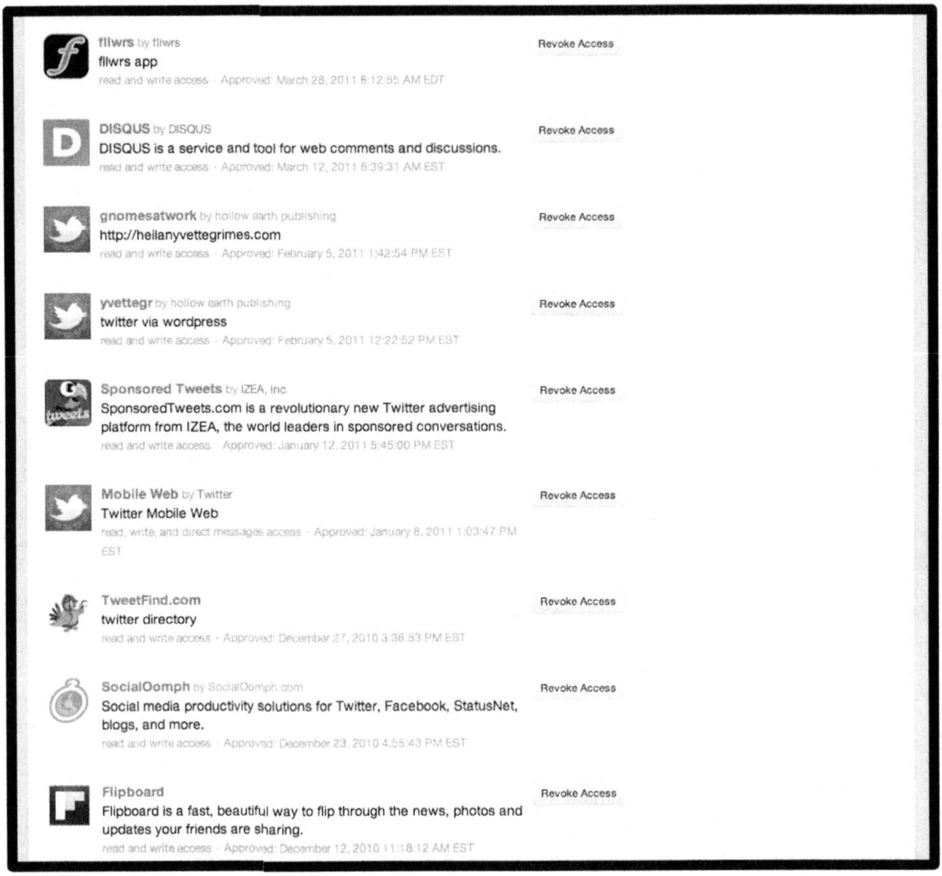
fllwrs by fllwrs
fllwrs app
read and write access · Approved: March 28, 2011 8:12:55 AM EDT
Revoke Access
DISQUS by DISQUS
DISQUS is a service and tool for web comments and discussions.
read and write access · Approved: March 12, 2011 6:39:31 AM EST
Revoke Access
gnomesatwork by hollow earth publishing
http://heilanyvettegrimes.com
read and write access · Approved: February 5, 2011 1:42:54 PM EST
Revoke Access
yvettegr by hollow earth publishing
twitter via wordpress
read and write access · Approved: February 5, 2011 12:22:52 PM EST
Revoke Access
Sponsored Tweets by IZEA, Inc
SponsoredTweets.com is a revolutionary new Twitter advertising platform from IZEA, the world leaders in sponsored conversations.
read and write access · Approved: January 12, 2011 5:45:00 PM EST
Revoke Access
Mobile Web by Twitter
Twitter Mobile Web
read, write, and direct messages access · Approved: January 8, 2011 1:03:47 PM EST
Revoke Access
TweetFind.com
twitter directory
read and write access · Approved: December 27, 2010 3:36:53 PM EST
Revoke Access
SocialOomph by SocialOomph.com
Social media productivity solutions for Twitter, Facebook, StatusNet, blogs, and more.
read and write access · Approved: December 23, 2010 4:55:43 PM EST
Revoke Access
Flipboard
Flipboard is a fast, beautiful way to flip through the news, photos and updates your friends are sharing.
read and write access · Approved: December 12, 2010 11:18:12 AM EST
Revoke Access

TweetBackup by Triop AB
Twitter backup web service
read and write access · Approved: December 8, 2010 7:43:52 PM EST
Revoke Access
historyapp by hollow earth publishing
This app is to make it easier to integrate my history tweeting with twitter.
read and write access · Approved: November 21, 2010 9:04:55 PM EST
Revoke Access
Futuretweets V2 by SolidFlux
The new and improved version of futuretweets.com
read and write access · Approved: October 25, 2010 12:20:27 AM EDT
Revoke Access
Whack!
Tweeter Karma by Dossy Shiobara
Tweeter Karma simplifies routine friend and follower management, offering different filters and sorting options for your entire account, all on one screen.
read and write access · Approved: October 16, 2010 3:39:01 PM EDT
Revoke Access
Flux by MTV Networks
Flux Twitter Application
read and write access · Approved: August 16, 2010 3:18:10 PM EDT
Revoke Access
Search - mzs by Home
The search.twitter.com app (to be renamed)
read and write access · Approved: August 3, 2010 7:12:27 PM EDT
Revoke Access
tm
TweetMeme by Favorit Ltd.
Tweetmeme is a service which aggregates all the popular links on Twitter to determine which links are popular.
read and write access · Approved: July 28, 2010 11:06:42 AM EDT
Revoke Access
login.getsatisfaction.com by Get Satisfaction
Allows you to link your twitter account to the Get Satisfaction website.
read and write access · Approved: July 15, 2010 5:14:11 PM EDT
Revoke Access
Twitter for iPhone by Twitter
Twitter for iPhone
read, write, and direct messages access · Approved: July 14, 2010 8:39:48 PM EDT
Revoke Access

Tweepi by ThoughtPick
Revoke Access
Tweepi is a simple collection of Twitter tools: Geeky Follow, Flush, Reciprocate and Cleanup - as well as more to come...
read and write access · Approved: June 12, 2010 4:11:04 PM EDT
Visibli by Visibli
Revoke Access
Your Content. Working for You.
read and write access · Approved: April 18, 2010 1:43:15 PM EDT
Twitpic by Twitpic Inc
Revoke Access
Share photos on Twitter with Twitpic
read and write access · Approved: April 17, 2010 11:25:55 AM EDT
UberMarket by UberMedia, Inc.
Revoke Access
Build your following, grow your influence.
read and write access · Approved: April 12, 2010 10:45:43 AM EDT
TweepML by TweepML
Revoke Access
TweepML is an simple way to create lists of Twitter users, and for people to search for interesting lists of users to follow several of them with a single-click.
read and write access · Approved: March 29, 2010 7:18:48 AM EDT
Ad.ly Network by Ad.ly Inc
Revoke Access
Ad.ly is an in-stream advertising platform that matches high value Twitter publishers with brands and agencies.
read and write access · Approved: March 27, 2010 6:29:42 PM EDT
PeopleBrowsr by PeopleBrowsr
Revoke Access
Online visual dashboard for your online identities
read and write access · Approved: March 27, 2010 6:24:53 PM EDT
TweetPhoto by TweetPhoto
Revoke Access
TweetPhoto is a real-time photo sharing platform for the social web.
read and write access · Approved: March 10, 2010 6:40:27 AM EST
Formspring.me by Formspring.me Inc
Revoke Access
Formspring is a service that allows your friends and followers to ask you questions, anonymous or not. You can respond to those questions and optionally publish responses to Twitter or your blog.
read and write access · Approved: March 7, 2010 10:02:13 AM EST

yfrog
Yfrog by ImageShack
Share your images and videos on Twitter!
read and write access · Approved: February 23, 2010 7:37:13 AM EST
Revoke Access
Twibes by Adam Loving
Twibes lets you vote for your favorite tweeters, create groups, and manage your followers.
read and write access · Approved: January 26, 2010 1:31:25 PM EST
Revoke Access
BigTweet
BigTweet by Scott Carter
BigTweet is a bookmarklet that lets you post to Twitter as you surf the web.
read and write access · Approved: January 18, 2010 9:40:34 AM EST
Revoke Access
The Whuffie Bank by The Whuffie Bank
Whuffies are a new type of social currency. Share them with your friends, colleagues and people you admire.
read and write access · Approved: January 17, 2010 6:30:21 AM EST
Revoke Access
Brizzly by Thing Labs
A simple way to experience the social web.
read and write access · Approved: January 15, 2010 3:29:45 PM EST
Revoke Access
Favstar.FM
Authorizing Favstar allows for your favorites and retweets to displayed in real time. Your stats will be updated more regularly. You can configure fav notifications on Favstar's settings screen.
read and write access · Approved: January 15, 2010 3:13:46 PM EST
Revoke Access
The Visitor Widget
The #1 Twitter statistics site.
read and write access · Approved: December 23, 2009 10:53:53 AM EST
Revoke Access
Listorious by Sawhorse Media
The directory of the most awesome lists on Twitter
read and write access · Approved: December 23, 2009 7:25:45 AM EST
Revoke Access
Twaitter by NOV, LLC
Twaitter is a web based Twitter client that enables you to schedule the messages you send and better manage your tweets through our message management tools.
read and write access · Approved: December 15, 2009 1:55:00 PM EST
Revoke Access
TweetGrid
Twitter Search Dashboard
TweetGrid for iPhone by TweetGrid.com
TweetGrid for iPhone and iPod Touch users!
read and write access · Approved: December 3, 2009 9:23:17 AM EST
Revoke Access
TL
Twitlonger by Stuart Gibson
Twitlonger is a simple app to allow you to post longer thoughts via Twitter, without the need to write a whole blog post. Think of it like Twitpic for text.
read and write access · Approved: November 24, 2009 1:17:45 PM EST
Revoke Access
Dynamic
Dynamic Tweets by Ei Dynamics
Automatically schedule and send tweets. Great for scheduled events, special promotional offerings, Twitter campaigns. Don't worry about forgetting to send a tweet anymore.
read and write access · Approved: September 25, 2009 8:33:15 AM EDT
Revoke Access
© 2011 Twitter About Us Contact Blog Status Resources API Business Help Jobs Terms Privacy

If you do revoke access the button turns into an "oops" button and you can immediately "Undo Revoke Access".

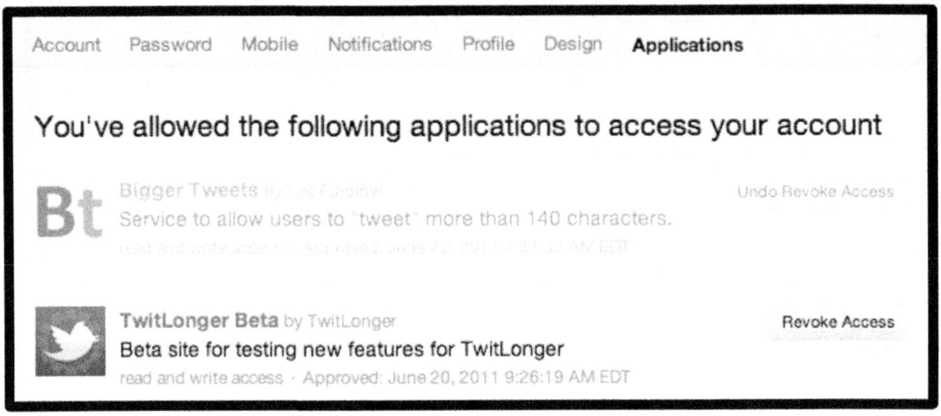

There is no Save button to the Applications tab. It's just an area where you can Revoke access to outside applications so no overall Save button is needed. Either you grant a Twitter provider access or revoke it. No save needed.

Now that you've got your Twitter account set up, it's time to figure out what to do with it and how Twitter works.

CHAPTER 4

USING TWITTER

WHAT IS A TWEET?

Each tweet you send is actually turned into an html page. Check it out by clicking on your tweet and you'll see the html page. You can copy the URL and send it as a link to highlight specific tweets.

Twitter does have limits on how many tweets you can send. The maximum is 1000 per day (a retweet is counted as a tweet). And you can't send them all at once. They have to be broken down throughout the day. A thousand should be more than enough to accommodate everything you have to say. Twitter Limits are discussed in Chapter 5 (see page 107).

TYPES OF TWEETS

There are three types of tweets:

Regular Tweet: Tweeted from your home page. It is public unless you've protected your tweets, in which case it is visible only to those you've granted access to your tweets.

Reply: A reply to a tweet someone else has made. The tweet appears in your twitterstream and the person you're responding to's twitterstream. If they've protected their tweets then your reply is private. If their twitterstream is public, then your reply is public.

DM (Direct Message): This is a private Direct Message to someone. It does not appear in either of your twitterstreams. In order to DM someone you must both mutually follow each other. For example, you can't send a DM to Lady Gaga unless she also follows you.

A DM is formatted with a DM or D tag at the beginning of the tweet followed by the [twitter_id] of the person you're DMing. For example:

```
DM @yvettegr Great hearing from you.
D @yvettegr Great hearing from you.
```

YOUR BEGINNING HOME PAGE

This is the starting home page after you've set up your account.

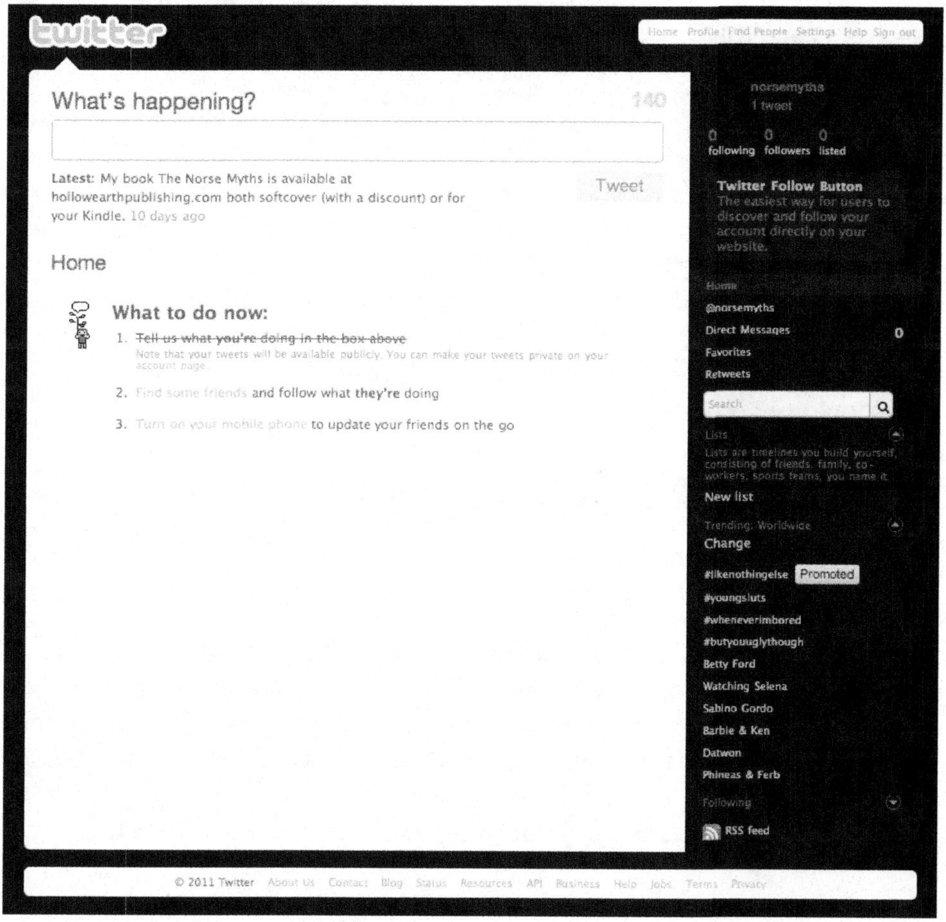

Note that I've already posted one tweet so the "Tell us what you're doing in the box above" is struck through, and you can see my First/Latest tweet under the What's Happening box.

YOUR FIRST TWEET

Your account is all set up, everything looks good, now you're ready for your first tweet. If you're like everyone else (myself included) it might go something like this:

Just trying to think what to tweet?

I joined Twitter on April 17, 2008. I was at a client's and a gentleman named Lee Dolby (thank you Lee) showed me a tweet on his mobile phone. I couldn't for the life of me understand why it would be useful. But, to be nice, I signed up, posted my first tweet about trying to decide what to tweet, and then did nothing for months and months. I believe my next tweet was that December about how my car was a block of ice. Then it was just a few tweets and months until I decided I liked history and should tweet about that.

WHY ARE YOU ON TWITTER?

What do you hope to do on twitter? Get lots of followers? Help others? Make money? Educate others? All of those things?

Once you figure out what you want to do on Twitter you'll be able to figure out how to do it. And that will help you know what to tweet. Remember no one, not even your family, owes you reading your tweets. You have to make people want to read them because they're interesting or useful. You can put them out there but don't expect people to automatically read them. But kudos to you for putting them out there.

WHAT TO TWEET

Personal Tweets

"I'm sitting on my porch right now!"

"Think I'll go to a movie."

Those kind of tweets are for family only and will not build you a following, unless you're already famous and people want to know what you're doing. But, if that's not the case your tweets have to be interesting. Interesting enough for someone to click that follow button. So what do you tweet?

If you find your tweets boring, chances are everyone else will, too. Tweet interesting, useful, things. Become part of the community.

Engage in conversation. If someone tweets something you like and you have a response, tweet them back. One advantage of replying to someone's tweet (and sending it publicly and not as a DM) is your comments are in their twitterstream and seen by their followers. And one of those followers might like your comments so much that they follow you.

Ask questions. Give quotes. Post links. Respond to questions. Be provocative. Do a giveaway. If you've got a book, then hold a Twitter contest. Who has the best answer to this? First person with a great hidden place to vacation gets my travel guide.

The best things to tweet are things you're interested in. Do you have a hobby? Are you passionate about paintings, museums, demolition derbies?

Right now, without any hesitation, what's your favorite thing in the world to do? Whatever you thought of might be something you could focus on tweeting about.

You'll be most successful on Twitter if you find your niche, something you're interested in and want to tell others about. Even if it's obscure, there will be others interested. It's better to have a 1000 targeted twitterers than 10,000 who have nothing in common with you. Sometimes it isn't about numbers.

You may not know at first what you want your Twitter account to be about. So, tweet what you want. Eventually you'll settle on your niche. Whether or not it proves to be popular, only time will tell.

You never know what's going to be popular. One of the most popular twitterstreams (with almost 2.5 million followers) is twitter.com/s**tmydadsays (the person's [twitter_id] uses the actual word). It's just some guy quoting his dad. Fortunately his dad has an interesting perspective on the world and his son and his twitterstream caught on. It has spawned books and even a sitcom starring William Shatner. I doubt when this guy started tweeting he ever thought he'd end up making a career at it and lots of money.

So, tweet what interests you, what you're passionate about. And if that passion comes through in your tweets you'll get followers. The worst thing to do is to pick a topic and tweet it because you think it'll be popular. You have to have a passion for the topic to begin with. Just deciding to do movie reviews when you don't like movies that much will result in a pretty boring twitterstream.

But, what if you really like ice cream. It's your passion. You make it. You go to ice cream shoppes and eat it. You're all over the web looking for recipes. Then that's your topic. And if you're that passionate about ice cream I guarantee it'll come through in your tweets. And you'll get followers.

Think of your hobbies. It can be anything. Do you crochet or knit? What about quilting? Or collecting something? Maybe you've got a BMW you work on and you go to Beamer events. These are things you could build a twitterstream around.

Ask a question, or put forth an observation and ask for comments. People like to engage in conversation. Give people a reason to read your tweets. Always write from the reader's perspective. How will reading your tweets help them? What do your tweets do for them? Do your tweets make them laugh, give them advice, link them to freebies? Be useful.

If you don't know something, ask. Ask for suggestions on computers or apps to buy? Ask for suggestions for books to read, etc. People like being helpful.

Say you're in a strange town and you don't know what to do for dinner or where to go for a movie or what museums are good. Ask. People will respond. However, don't say something like, "Great, I like that restaurant suggestion, I think I'll go there this evening for dinner." You might find some people have decided to join you. How will they know it's you. Your tweet has implied you're alone. They go to the restaurant looking for someone seated alone. Or, you might be tweeting. They might even tweet asking you if you found the restaurant all right and then they'll look around to see who is answering a tweet. Be careful. You don't really want to broadcast your whereabouts on Twitter.

This does bring up the general question of being too specific about your whereabouts. That's why I turn off the geolocation feature on Twitter. It puts location information with your Tweet. TMI. Also not a good idea to say you're going to be on vacation for a week, or out of town for the weekend. There are stories of people doing that and then having people who knew them slightly and knew where they lived break into their home and take their time cleaning the place out since they knew their friend was out of town, maybe even tweeting what fun they were having on vacation. And they could check by looking at their tweets on Twitter or actually sending them a DM asking how their vacation was going and what they were doing? Be careful. It's social media, not friends-and-family-I-can-trust-everyone-media. Maintain some privacy.

Remember you can have several twitterstreams. You might want one that's personal and you don't particularly want it to grow beyond family and friends. The private one you can talk about your vacation or meeting everyone for a movie. Just make certain to change your password every month. You could have a public twitterstream focused on your hobby and something you want to grow with as many targeted followers as possible.

If you have lots of hobbies then have lots of twitterstreams. And you could have a twitterstream for business.

Just make certain you're tweeting about things that interest you. You won't get bored, your enthusiasm will shine through, and you'll get followers, even if it's the most obscure topic in the world.

TRENDING TOPICS

Another way to come up with good, effective tweets, is to look at the Trending Topics on Twitter. These are the topics that are the most popular at the moment as defined by number of people tweeting using a #hashtag for a topic. To find Trending Topics just hit the Home menu button in the upper right of your Twitter screen and then look down the right sidebar. There will be a section showing Trending Topics. Next to the word "Trending" is the area you've selected to narrow down trends. By default this will be the largest city near your profile city. You can click the "Change" underneath "Trending" to change this to another city or country. I wish as an option in the future Twitter also let you select Trending Topics for subject categories. I'm not particularly interested in what is Trending in Boston. But I am interested in what is trending in Publishing, Fibromyalgia, and other topics. I think that would be much more valuable than Trending Topics by City.

STILL CAN'T THINK WHAT TO TWEET?

Quotes appropriate to the day or what's going on in the news are always good. There are a lot of quote sites on the web where you can find appropriate tweets.

Tweet inspirational messages. Quotes from the Bible, about Gandhi, Lincoln, inspiring people or events.

Humorous quotes. Mark Twain comes to mind.

Tweet about others you find interesting.

Tweet about deals. Find some freebie websites and tweet daily links to free stuff. Give advice on couponing and saving money. Google "Free Stuff on the internet". This should give you quite a bit to tweet about.

You could post some original tweets but mostly retweet other tweets you find interesting.

Go on YouTube and find instructional videos, or health videos, cute kitten videos. Build your twitterstream from YouTube videos. Of the topics I've mentioned, you'll have the greatest success with cute kittens. Winner all the way. Never underestimate the public's love of cute kittens. That's your goto tweet/video. After that little chipmunks and gerbils eating celery. People will watch videos like that for hours and retweet them to their followers. Twitter gold.

Hold contests. Once you get a fairly large following you can get companies to give you merchandise to give away in contests. This is good because it gives the merchant advertising and it gives you something to give away to build your following. In order to enter twitterers would have to send you a Direct Message (DM). Of course, the only way to send you a DM is if you both mutually follow each other. So the person has to follow you first before being able to enter the contest.

MAKE YOUR TWEETS SOMETHING READERS LOOK FORWARD TOO

Make your postings daily affairs. Find a theme or niche and then split it up into special days. Monday, This; Tuesday, That. Make every day specific to a topic. People may read every day, but at the least will definitely find at least one day to look forward to your tweets.

Be an authority twitterstream. Professionally, or as a hobby, there are things you know a great deal about. Set yourself up on Twitter as an authority. Tweet confidently. You'll gain a following if you know what you're tweeting about, or at least convince others that you do. Twitterers will look forward to specific information. This is great if you are trying to be an authority twitterstream.

SHOULD YOU BE CONTROVERSIAL?

Whether or not you're controversial depends on the nature of your twitterstream. If you're taking sides in politics, then it would be hard to avoid being controversial. If you're tweeting about children's birthday parties then probably best to leave the controversy elsewhere. Use your common sense. Is it appropriate to be controversial based on the tone of your overall twitterstream? Will you shock your followers so much by being out of character that they'll wonder what happened to you?

It's okay to be provocative and forceful in your opinions. Take sides. Are you a Liberal? Conservative? Then explain your positions and the news in 140-character increments. Be fair. The other side will try to use your tweets against you. Some just want to change your mind but won't even entertain the thought of changing their mind. Just keep it friendly and exchange ideas.

Are you going to be all about the controversy? Then do so. If you're going to take a political point of view then do so. Then people will expect it. But if you are tweeting jokes and fun things don't all of a sudden tweet provocative things that are out of character for your twitterstream. People are following you for specific reasons. Don't surprise them too much. Don't disappoint them at all.

BUSINESS TWEETS

Twitter has no prohibitions against businesses promoting and selling things on Twitter. What you must not do is spam people or engage in selling fraudulent products or schemes.

Don't be selling all the time. Give people a break once in a while and talk about other things. A soft sell works much better than a hard sell on Twitter. Since you've got only 140-characters you should have a product page you can link to that has the description and order information about your product.

TWITIQUETTE

Twitiquette (also twetiquette) is etiquette on Twitter. The Golden Rule applies on Twitter too. Do until others as you would have them do unto you. If they follow you, follow them back. It's common courtesy. If they retweet you then find something to retweet of theirs. Maybe not immediately, but at some point. If they DM you or mention you in their twitterstream, answer them, even if only to thank them.

WHAT NOT TO TWEET

Read Your Tweet Before You Send It

It's only 140-characters max, so take the time to read your tweet before you send it. Check for misspelled words and grammar/punctuation errors. Check any facts (don't make things up). And if you've included a link, test the link to make certain it works.

Don't Spam

It's okay to sell things on Twitter, but make certain what you're selling is legitimate. The nice thing is that Twitter does not allow you to send the same message over and over. So, if you're going to try to spam you have to change the words a bit from message to message. Since Twitter only searches back two weeks, chances are you can resend messages from two weeks ago.

Don't Post Lots of Tweets Seconds Apart

First it's irritating to others. Second, it looks like spam to Twitter. You might have noticed I have almost 37,500 tweets. When I was posting a lot I would space my tweets at five-minute intervals. You don't want to make people so mad that they unfollow you. People who follow me know that sometimes they're going to get a lot of tweets. But, these are informational tweets, and certainly not spam.

Don't Cuss, Be Polite

Cussing turns people off. But you say in real life you cuss like a sailor? Then do that. Cuss in real life. But if you want to be popular on Twitter, don't cuss. Don't yell at people. Say thank you. If someone is kind enough to comment or retweet you, acknowledge them with a thank you. This is called manners. Common courtesy is something good to do for no other reason that it is good to do. People like positive, kind people more than they like angst ridden jerks.

Be careful how you write. Not much emotion in writing, particular at 140-characters a tweet. You might think you're being clever, everyone else might think you're being smarmy. What might seem normal for you in everyday conversation probably looks very cold when written out. Jokes are the hardest things to tweet. Time after time you see people getting into trouble and having to apologize for being misunderstood and that they were just trying to be funny.

Don't Insult People

You can disagree, but do it without calling people names. You've really lost the argument once you descend into name-calling. And you just look silly when you start comparing others to Hitler. So, don't do that.

SHARE THE LOVE: WHY RETWEETING IS IMPORTANT

The biggest compliments on Twitter are to be followed and to be retweeted. You want both. If you find someone else's twitterstream interesting, then tell others about it. Even put it in one of your lists. When people see you sharing the love for others they'll share the love for you, if you have interesting informative tweets.

When you're retweeted your tweet appears in that person's twitterstream. And that person has people who don't know you and don't follow you. They might find your tweet interesting and follow you.

For some odd reason I've found a tweet is more likely to get retweeted in the morning than afternoon or evening. I refer to these as coffee retweets. People are having their breakfast, sipping their morning coffee, lazily reading Twitter and retweeting. It's a lazy way for them to post interesting things on their twitterstream without doing much work. The vast majority of my retweets occur in the morning. This means you have to be tweeting in the morning or using a tweet scheduler client (see page 178).

There's something called a "call to action". That's when you ask someone to do something. So saying "Please RT" is a call to action. You think what you've tweeted is important enough to ask people to retweet it. I don't usually do this because it smacks of desperation. Let your tweet/retweet speak for itself. If it's worth retweeting, it'll get retweeted. The major exception being in times of disaster when you want to urgently get the word out about something.

Putting "twitthis" in your tweet is also a call to action, and the same as putting "Please RT" in your tweet.

#HASHTAGS

This "#" is a hashtag. You use this to tag your tweet as belonging to a specific event or topic on Twitter so that your tweet will be included when someone searches on that topic. Anyone can create a hashtag. Whether or not it becomes popular for a day or an ongoing hashtag depends on the whims of people on Twitter.

Hashtags can use words, names, or abbreviations/acronyms. For example #gno is the hashtag for "girls night out" so you can't really use it for anything else that uses gno as an abbreviation or acronym.

How to Set Up a Hashtag

Your hashtag might already be in use. If it's an acronym it might already have a meaning different than how you want to use it. Check at hashtags.org to see if it's already being used for something. This is also the place to find official hashtags. Well, official in the sense that everyone agrees to the parameters set by hashtags.org.

In order for your hashtag to work and be listed at hashtags.org you must go to twitter.com/hashtags and follow them. Then put the "#" sign before the term you want to use as a hashtag.

Be specific in your hashtags. "#washington" is too general. It could be Washington state, Washington D.C., or even George Washington. And you might have meant to use it for Washington University.

Keep your hashtag short since it counts as part the 140-character limit in your tweet. If you use an acronym make certain its something familiar enough that people will know it.

/SLASHTAGS

/Slashtags use the solidus/virgule/forward slash/slasher to set off some metadata about a tweet, usually that it is being sent via someone. For example,

> The beginning of the tweet /via @twitter1 /by @twitter2 /cc twitter3.

MORE TWITTER COMMANDS

There's a whole bunch of Twitter commands you can use to define your tweets. You can send a tweet privately, suggesting to someone they update their home page, even designate a tweet as a favorite. Some you'll be familiar with, others you'll find more obscure. Some you've probably never heard of. The first one is the standard Twitter tag to send someone a message.

@[twitter_id] This is a message I'm sending you.

What this command does is send a public message to another twitterer. The message appears in both your twitterstreams. If you've protected your tweets then it's a private message seen only by those you've approved to see your messages.

DM @[twitter_id] This is a private message I'm sending you.

D @[twitter_id] This is a private message I'm sending you.

DM stands for direct message. This is a private message sent from you to just one other person. You both have to be mutually following each other. If you follow that person and they don't follow you back then you'll receive a Twitter message telling you that you can't send a Direct Message to that person because they don't follow you.

Originally you had to use DM in front of the @[twitter_id]. Now you can just use a "D". But make certain that the @[twitter_id] follows the D. If you put the D after the @[twitter_id] then you'll just be sending a public message with a "D" at the beginning of it.

WHOIS @[twitter_id]

Type this in the tweet field and then hit tweet.

The twitterer's [twitter_id] along with the month and year they joined Twitter appears followed by their profile information.

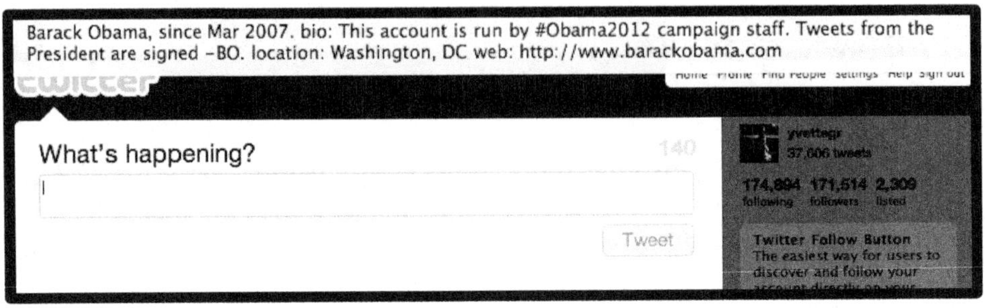

GET @[twitter_id]

Type GET @[twitter_id] in the tweet field and then hit tweet. That person's most recent tweet appears.

NUDGE @[twitter_id]

This sends a nudge to the twitterer reminding them to update their twitterstream since they haven't posted in a while.

FAV @[twitter_id]

Typing this in your Twitter field and then hitting the tweet button to post it marks this twitterer's last tweet as a favorite. If they've just posted and you reply to that post with FAV @[twitter_id] it will be marked as a favorite.

STATS

Just type the word STATS in the tweet field and then hit the tweet button and Twitter will return your stats: how many people you're following, number of followers, which words (if any) that you're tracking. This does not appear as a tweet in your twitterstream when you hit the tweet button.

INVITE [phone number]

This will send an SMS text message to the phone number after INVITE. And remember don't use the brackets when you tweet this.

LISTS

One way to get followers is to be mentioned on lists. This is because people will see an interesting list and follow everyone on that list by just clicking on one button. So, if you're on a popular list you'll get a lot of followers just by being on the list.

Other twitterers have to decide to put you on their list. And lists are usually topic specific. If you do movie reviews don't expect to be on a list for flower arranging.

You should make your own lists. But do not put yourself on your own lists. All of your tweets will show up in the lists and crowd out everyone else. Since you own the list people already know about you so it's unnecessary to include yourself on lists you create.

Lists are also a way of organizing how you read tweets. You can group specific people or topics into a list and easily go through that list to read the latest tweets by those in that list. You can create lists on as many topics as you want. Make them very specific. Instead of automobiles, make it a list about a specific make of automobile. Instead of a list of Things to Do, make it more specific to your area, Things to do in Northeastern Ohio, or Things to do in Cleveland.

If you have interesting lists and people like your list topics they will probably follow to you just because of your lists.

Secret Twitter List Feature: Follow Recommendations

If you want to share the love and create a list of Follow Recommendations for those who follow you. What that means if someone follows you they'll receive your list, and your list consists of names of your favorite twitterers they should follow. Here's a very easy way to do it. It's a really neat Twitter Trick.

- Go to your Lists dropdown menu and select "New List" and name it something unique. I named mine "Hi from Yvettegr"

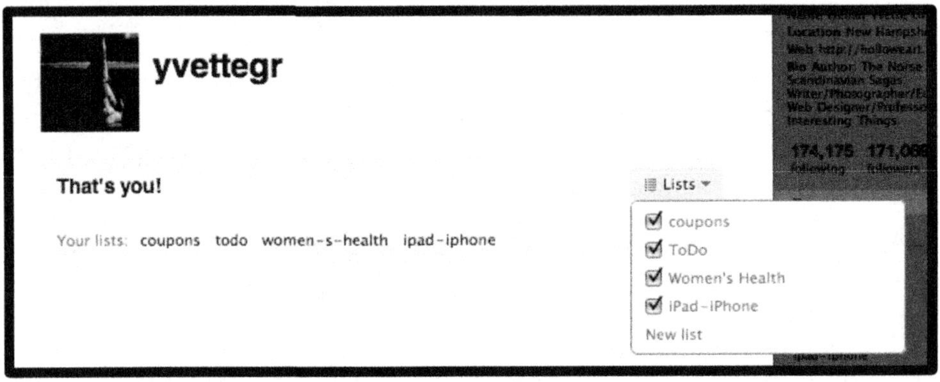

- In the description field write something like:
- Thanks for the follow. Here are some twitterers I think you might like: #twitterers
- Of course, write whatever you like above, and use whatever hashtag you want to define your group.
- Make your list public.

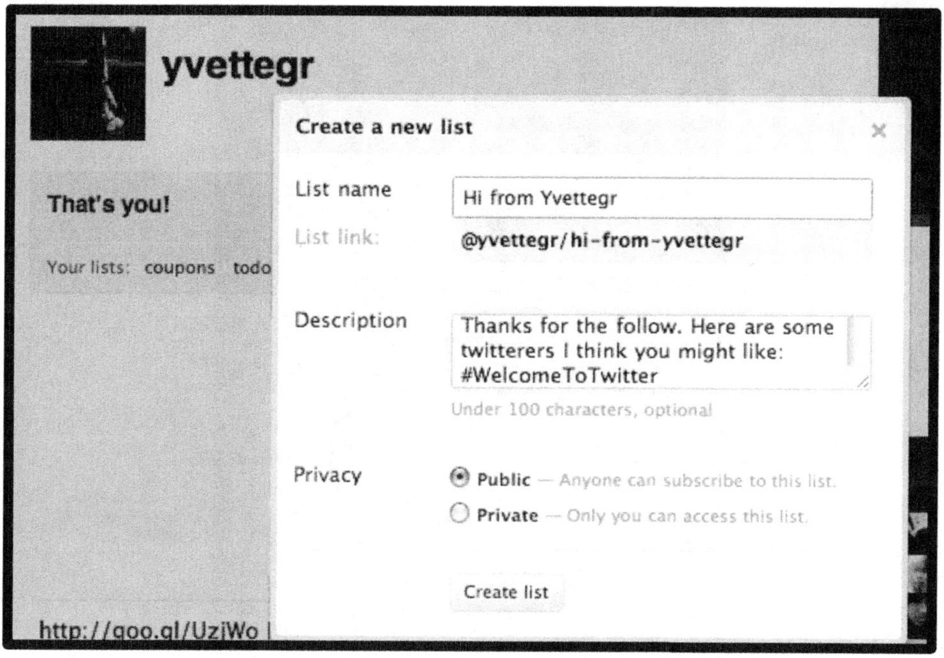

- Hit "Create list" and your list will show up in the sidebar with your other lists.

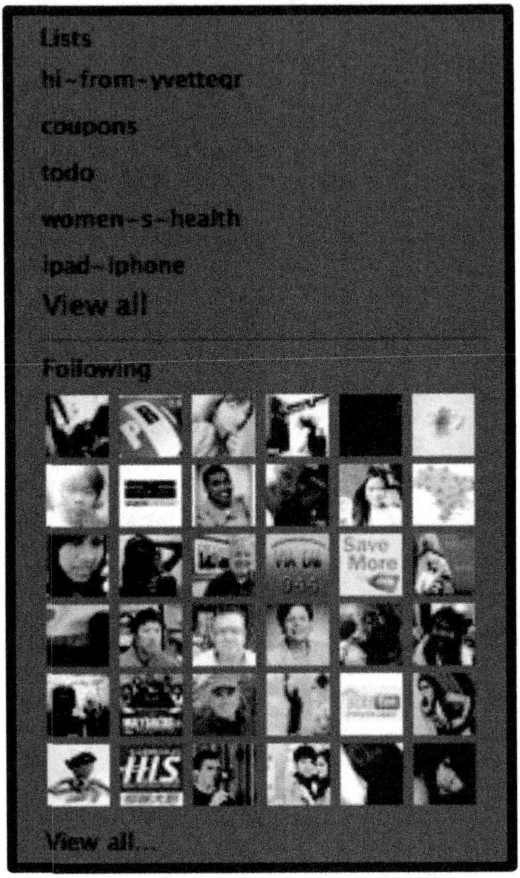

- Then add people to this list. You can go through your followers and add those you want to recommend. Or you can add others on Twitter that you think are interesting. They actually don't have to be following you to be added to your list. You can recommend anyone. If you click on your list in the sidebar a Search window will pop up. You can search for a [twitter_id], first or last name, business, brand, or topic (search term). Much like you can with any list you create. This list is different because when someone follows you this list is sent to them.

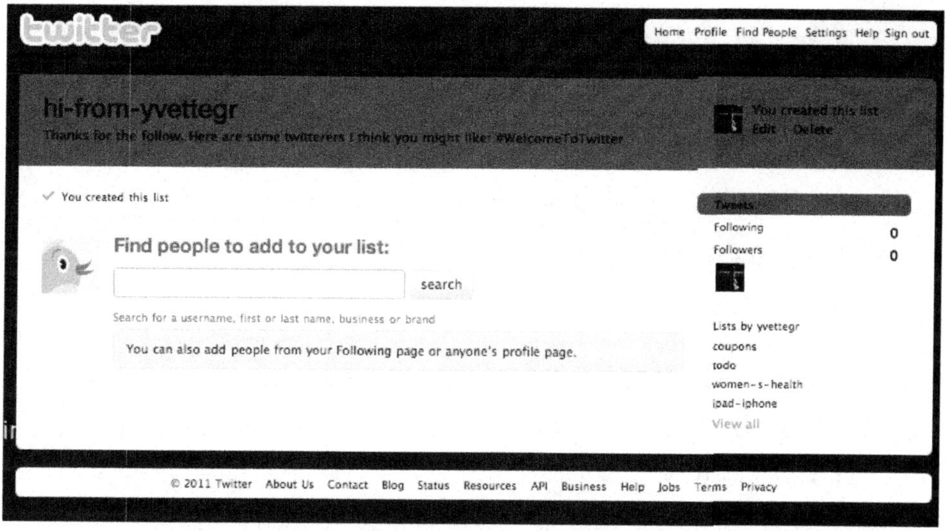

- When someone follows you they will get the "Hi from Yvettegr" list. They can hit the "Follow this list" button and automatically follow everyone on the list.
- This is a great way to give back and show some love to your favorite followers, or favorite people on Twitter whether they follow you or not.

USING FORMULISTS TO MAKE SELF-UPDATING TWITTER LISTS

Formulists

formulists.com

It is very easy to make self-updating lists. However the lists that Formulists creates are very limited in content.

First use Twitter's OAuth validation to sign into Formulists with your Twitter account.

After you've given Formulists access to your Twitter account you'll be taken to the next page. There's a nice video tutorial called "Getting Started with Formulists" by Formulists. Watch it. It's only 27 seconds long. Essentially it gives you all the steps you need:

- Click on "Add a Forumlists List"
- Select a category
- Choose a list from the category
- Name your list and customize for list-specific features
- Select basic list options (size, public or private) and write a Description of your list.
- Add any filtering options (location, bio, followers, etc.)
- Create and check out your lists on Twitter (or the Twitterclient you might be using)

And that's it. You have a list. Formulists will update it for 2 months. In order to keep Formulists updating your lists you have to log on every two months. If the list goes inactive longer than two months then Formulists deletes it. You do have the option of paying a $0.99 monthly fee for their premium service. It gives you the ability to create up to 20 lists and no need to logon every two months.

USING TWITTER ON YOUR MOBILE PHONE

If you can type in URL's on your mobile phone then you can go to twitter.com and tweet from there. Usually the mobile version will pop up. However there are several mobile Twitter clients you can use (see page 187). Probably the best is available free from Twitter. Twitter has versions that support most mobile phone platforms.

HOW TO GET TO 140 CHARACTERS

140 characters isn't a lot. Sometimes you just about make it, but still go over. There are things you can do to shorten your tweet:

You can always abbreviate words. I've included a list of abbreviations and smiley's (emoticons) you can use in your tweets (see page 199). This is just a basic list. I will have a book coming out in a few weeks that has a comprehensive list of abbreviations and smiley's. You can always email me about it.

- Leave out words like "the". You'll get used to it. Just make certain your tweet still makes sense.
- Use numerals instead of spelling out numbers: one = 1; twelve = 12. Writing out something like "one-hundred-and-twenty-seven" as 127 will save you a lot of characters.
- Instead of "and" use the ampersand &
- R instead of "are"
- U instead of "you"

Start reading lots of tweets and you'll realize what works and what doesn't work.

LINK SHORTENERS

You'll often provide a link to another webpage. Links can sometimes be absurdly long so you'll want to use a link shortener. Because of Twitter's 140-character limit Twitter suggests you use link shorteners to compact links. And in case you don't get the hint if you include a long URL in your tweet, Twitter will automatically shorten the links. There are lots of link shorteners to choose from (see page 167).

t.co

t.co is Twitter's link shortener. You just paste in your URL and when you hit send Twitter will automatically shorten the link to no more than nineteen characters. However, they do not provide any analytics. And if you don't like to use their link shortener you may use whatever one you want. They have not blocked any link shorteners.

goo.gl

I've used quite a few link shorteners but have pretty much settled on goo.gl because I like Google, and I like the analytics and tracking available for my tweets. Also, I know Google isn't going anywhere so my URL's will be active next year. Some link shorteners I've used have abandoned old links and when I clicked on an old tweet I found it is no longer linked to the original file. The link shortener automatically deleted the link after a while.

Now for a really useful hint about putting a shortened link in your tweet. Put the shortened link at the start of your tweet. Then the rest of your tweet should deal with what the link is about. The reason for this is if you've put the link at the end of your tweet (like just about everyone does) and your tweet is retweeted and the retweet makes your tweet go over the 140-character limit your link will be truncated making it useless. If your link is at the start of your tweet and the retweet goes beyond 140-characters then the end of your tweet is cut off but the important link is okay.

LINKING PHOTOS AND VIDEOS ON TWITTER

At some point you're going to want to tweet a link for a photo or video. Unfortunately, Twitter doesn't automatically show photos/videos. Instead you have to use a photo client where you've uploaded the photo/video, and then send the URL for that photo/video in your tweet. Photo clients can also automatically tweet any photos/videos you upload to Twitter (or facebook and other social networking sites). You can input a message with the tweet or not.

The three services I use the most are twitpic, yfrog, and mobypicture. I use three photoclients so I can sort out the photos/videos I upload. I post general news images and videos that I want to tweet to others on twitpic. I upload my personal photos and videos that I want to tweet on yfrog. And I use mobypicture to upload client photos to tweet. It's just a way of keeping my personal photos/videos separate from general news photos/videos and client photos/videos.

By having my personal photos/videos concentrated together on yfrog I have a nice online portfolio. I can send my yfrog link to people and they can scroll through the photos/videos I've uploaded. You can also send links to your other photo clients so people can scroll through all the photos/videos you've uploaded.

Was there any reason why I used twitpic for news/general photos, yfrog for personal photos, and mobypicture for client photos? No. I started using twitpic first and used it for everything so I couldn't really send a link to show people my photos separately. Then I heard about yfrog, and mobypicture. At that point I decided to separate my photos into categories and so kept twitpic for general usage, and yfrog and mobypicture for personal and client photos/videos.

HOW TO SIGN ON TO THESE SERVICES

When you use one of these services you login with your email address and password, or via Twitter OAuth validation. If you login via Twitter you do not have to give them your login or password. Click logon/signup and the photo client uses Twitter's OAuth verification. That way the photo client can post your photo/video URL and tweet via that photo client without them having access to your password. Anytime you want to revoke access you can go to your Twitter settings, and then to the Applications button and you'll see a list of all applications you've given permissions to. You can hit the Revoke Access button next to their name and they will no longer have access to your account. If you accidentally hit the Revoke Access button by mistake for an application you can immediately hit Undo Revoke Access. Once you've revoked access and clicked out of the Applications section, you have to go back to the original website of the photo client and give them access again if you want to use them.

Your photo/video does not actually appear on Twitter. Just the URL that links back to the photo client. Your photo stays on the Photo Client in your login section until you delete it. Photo Clients also give you statistics on how many people have viewed your photo, and how many days since you uploaded it.

Most of the photo clients work similarly and are very easy to use. Twitpic is by far the most popular.

Here's a list of the most popular photo/video clients. They all work pretty much the same:

- twitpic.com (the most popular)
- yfrog.com
- mobypicture.com
- snaptweet.com
- pikchur.com
- tweet.pho.to
- tweetphoto.com
- twitgoo.com
- twitlens.com
- twitsnaps.com
- twitxr.com
- Bubbletweet.com

twitpic

twitpic.com

You can create an account or login via Twitter OAuth verification. You can post from your computer, phone, or via email. Twitpic accepts GIF, JPG, or PNG images up to 10MB in size, and video up to 1:30 seconds in length. You can post a message with your uploaded photo or video. The message can only be 114 characters in length since the rest of Twitter's 140-characters is taken up with the photo/video Twitpic URL link. You do not have to automatically send a message to Twitter when you post your photo/video. You can just upload it and then send the URL to Twitter later in a tweet. Twitpic also has a photo widget you can use to post the photos you've uploaded to twitpic to your website or blog. Most Twitter clients work with twitpic.

Yfrog

yfrog.com

You can create an account or login via Twitter OAuth verification. Yfrog shows threaded replies from your Twitter account. You can follow and comment on Twitter from your yfrog account. Also shows your recently posted links. You can post from your computer, phone, or via email. You can upload GIF, JPG, BMP, or PNG images. Supported video formats are: flv, mpeg, mkv, wmv, mov, 3gp, mp4 avi, and several others. You can post a message with your uploaded photo or video.

mobypicture

mobypicture.com

You can create an account or login via Twitter OAuth verification. Mobypicture works with micro-blogs (Twitter, Tumblr, Brightkite, ovi, Jaiku); Social Networks (facebook, Hyves); Blogging platforms (Wordpress, Livejournal, Blogger); Media sites (Flickr, YouTube,

Vimeo). Other sites include Foursquare, StudiVZ, Hyves, Zideo, DeLoads, #at5, Autojunk, and NUfoto. You can send photos/videos from your iPhone, Android, Blackberry, Nokia, and website. And you can also upload via email.

picplz

picplz.com

Connect with facebook or Twitter and share your photos. Free apps from the Apple app store or Android store. The apps also include several photo effects you can apply to your photos before you upload them to Twitter (facebook).

snaptweet

snaptweet.com

This services allows you to share your Flickr pictures on Twitter.

Pikchur

pikchur.com

You can upload your photos/videos to pikchur and automatically share to several blogging and social media accounts including: Twitter, tumblr, facebook, friendfeed, flickr, Plurk, brightkite, identi.ca, jaiku, Totspo, OVi, Posterous, and Koornk.

Free and pro accounts available. Pro accounts give you an ad free account, expanded profile, Badge, larger photosize, Statistics, and Higher quality image rendering.

Tweetphoto

tweet.pho.to

You can share photos/videos to Twitter and facebook. This service does have an online photoeditor. You can also send your photos as an ecard to someone's email address using one of their many themes.

Twitgoo

twitgoo.com

Signin from your Twitter account using OAuth verification. The look and feel of the site resembles Twitter. This site is an extension of Photobucket.com so, obviously, it works best if you have a Photobucket account.

twitlens

twitlens.com

You can create an account or login via Twitter OAuth verification. Twitlens offers free accounts. You can upload up to 10 photos/videos at a time. Videos can be up to 50 mb in size. Photos/videos can show up as a tweet in your Twitter account. However, you have the option of an anonymous upload that does not show up in your twitterstream. Instead you can upload a photo/video and then privately share the URL with family and friends. If there are lots of people in your photos and they have Twitter accounts, you can tag your photos and they will be notified that they've been tagged in a photo.

Twitsnaps

twitsnaps.com

You can create an account or login via Twitter OAuth verification. Twitsnaps is a free service to share snaps and videos on Twitter. Fairly straightforward photo/video Twitter sharing service. They do give you statistics about the photos/videos you've uploaded.

twitxr

twitxr.com

Share your photos/videos on Twitter, facebook, flickr, and Picassa, directly from your mobile phone. Phones include: Apple iPhone, Windows Mobile, Nokia and Motorola, any other mobile phone via email.

Bubbletweet

bubbletweet.com

A special mention for bubbletweet.com. This lets you add a quick video to your tweet in the form of a popup round bubble. Unique. It's a way to add very short messages to your twitterstream.

Twitzer

twitzer.com

Twitzer.com links to shorttext.com. It goes beyond just posting images to Twitter. The site allows you to create a URL with some text (including rich text), image link, or video link without having a website. You can tweet the URL for the post to Twitter or elsewhere and link what you've written and the photos/videos. It's a nice way to quickly create a content link without having to post it on a website or blog. You can make your link private, if you wish and just share with specific individuals.

MORE PHOTO/VIDEO CLIENTS

Below are some more photo/video clients. But they seem to have a layer of complexity to them because they are doing more than just uploading to Twitter or facebook:

- flickr.com (photo sharing site)
- autopostr.com (works with your flickr.com account)
- brightkite.com
- friendfeed.com
- ping.fm
- posterous.com
- tumblr.com
- twitc.com

YOUTUBE

You don't need a photo client to tweet your YouTube videos. You can copy your YouTube URL, then use a link shortener since the YouTube link is fairly long (see pages 89 and 167), and then just tweet that URL to send readers to your youtube video. When you post your YouTube URL make certain you are on the video rather than your channel page. Otherwise if you change the video on your channel page the link will not show the video you want to show. And when you use a link shortener you don't have to copy the entire YouTube link. Here's an example of the URL for one of my videos:

http://www.youtube.com/watch?
v=_xlBegV_Rag&feature=channel_video_title

You can get rid of anything from the ampersand on:

http://www.youtube.com/watch?v=_xlBegV_Rag

The above works just as well as the example before it.

POSTING PHOTOS/VIDEOS THROUGH YOUR BROWSER

Check your browser extensions/addons to see if they have any Twitter clients. Firefox is particularly rich in Twitter extensions (addons) and is a superb browser.

UPLOADING PHOTOS AND VIDEOS FROM YOUR IPHONE, ANDROID PHONE, OR SMARTPHONE.

Every Twitter mobile app allows you to add a photo/video from your gallery, or take a new photo/video, to tweet. They work pretty much the same way. You open your mobile Twitter app, click on the new tweet or reply button, write a description if you want, and then click on the camera icon to select a photo or video from your gallery, or to take a new photo/video. After you select the photo/video you just hit send and a link for your photo or video appears in your tweet on Twitter.

MONETIZING TWITTER

Ad.ly

ad.ly

There are several monetizing companies that will find and place ads on your twitterstream. However, you won't earn much from most of them. In an entire month you might earn the cost of a cup of coffee.

However there is one service that pays fairly decently. And that's ad.ly. You sign up and choose the categories that best fit your twitterstream. Potential advertisers decide whom to use for advertising based on category selections.

If someone chooses you then you'll receive an email from ad.ly with the contents of the ad. You have the option to approve or disapprove the ad. If you approve then ad.ly will place the ad at the timeframe mentioned in the email.

Ad.ly pays based on how many followers you have, which is logical. The more followers you have the greater your reach and the more likely more of those followers will respond to the ad.

As far as advertisers are concerned, "CONTENT IS KING." If you have a lot of followers, but you tweet stupid messages, then don't expect to get a high-end company unless they want to appeal to your follower base. If they're a company trying to appeal to the business market they wouldn't be interested in you. Likewise if you have a super-serious twitterstream you're not likely to have a lot of young followers. Those wanting to appeal to that demographic will probably skip your twitterstream.

But you can make money using ad.ly. I'm just waiting for Twitter to let me put google adsense going down that right-hand sidebar.

TWITTER MESSAGE SCREENS

Twitter has quite a few message screens, the most famous of which is the Fail Whale. Here are all the screens I've managed to find.

Fail Whale (Over Capacity)

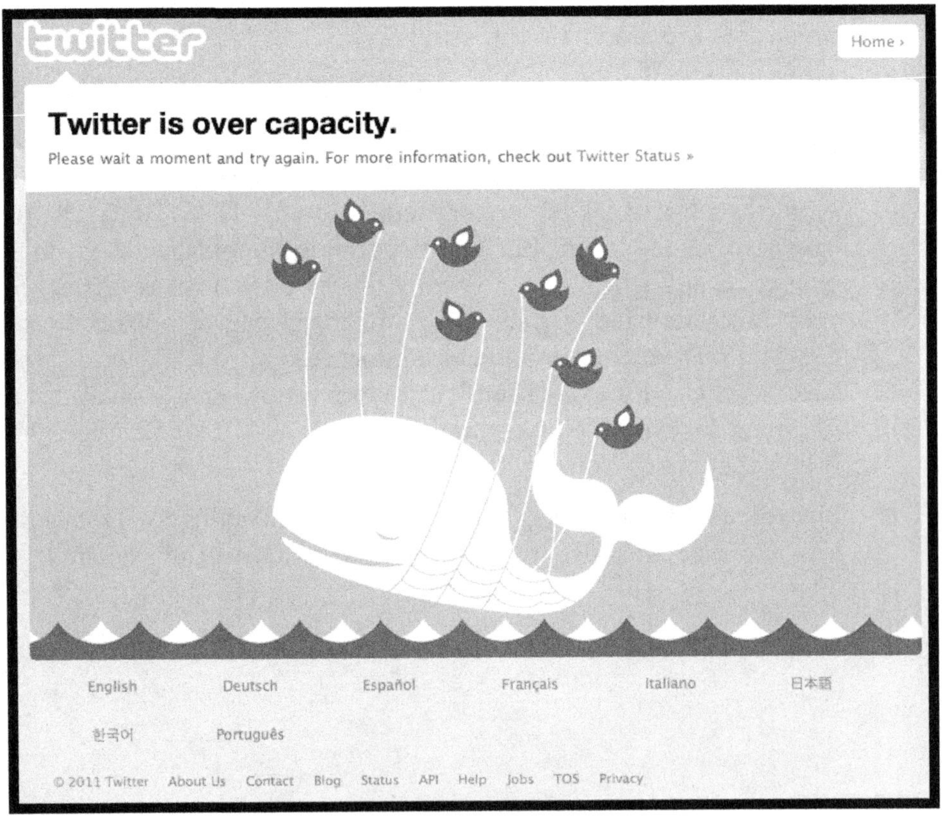

Foul Owl (Suspended Account)

This account is suspended.

This account is currently suspended and is being investigated due to strange activity.

If this is your account, or for more information about why an account may be suspended, see Suspended Accounts.

Home Help Contact Support

Profile Suspended

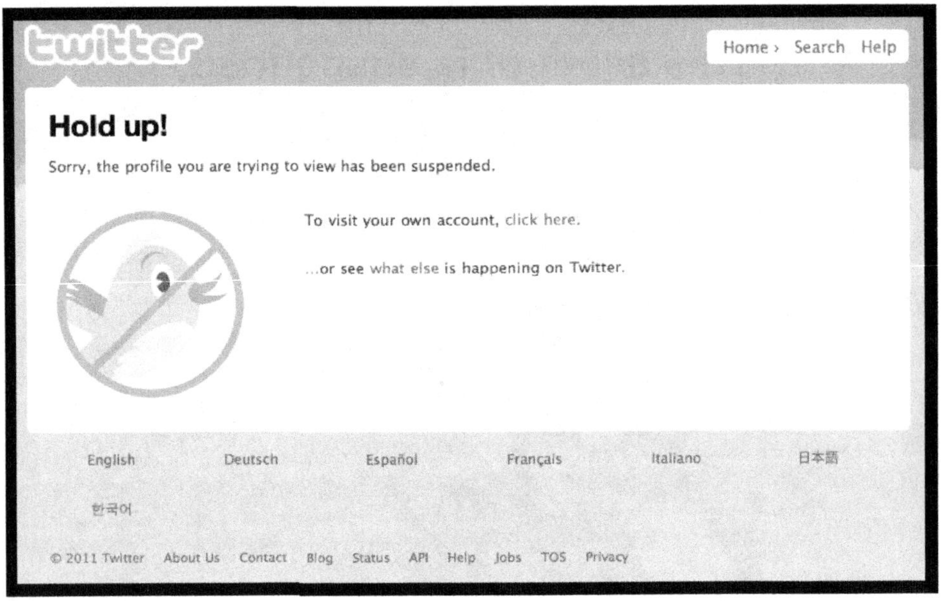

Couldn't Find Link

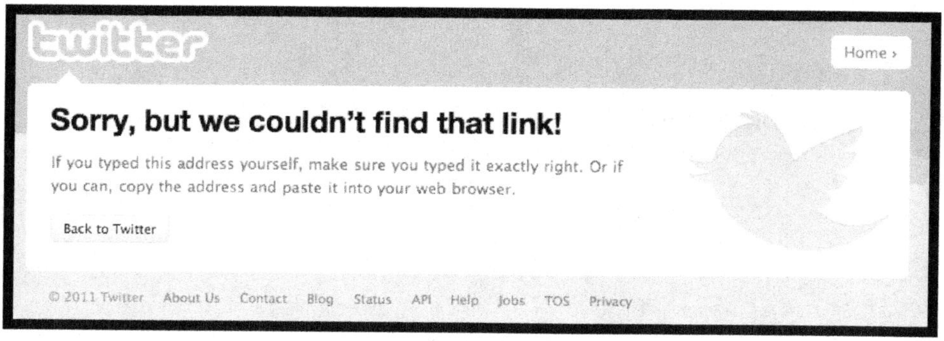

Page Doesn't Exist

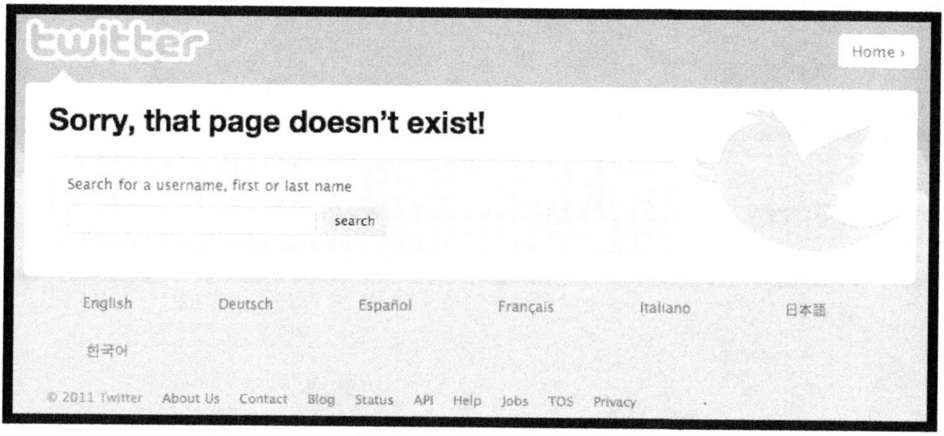

Something is Technically Wrong

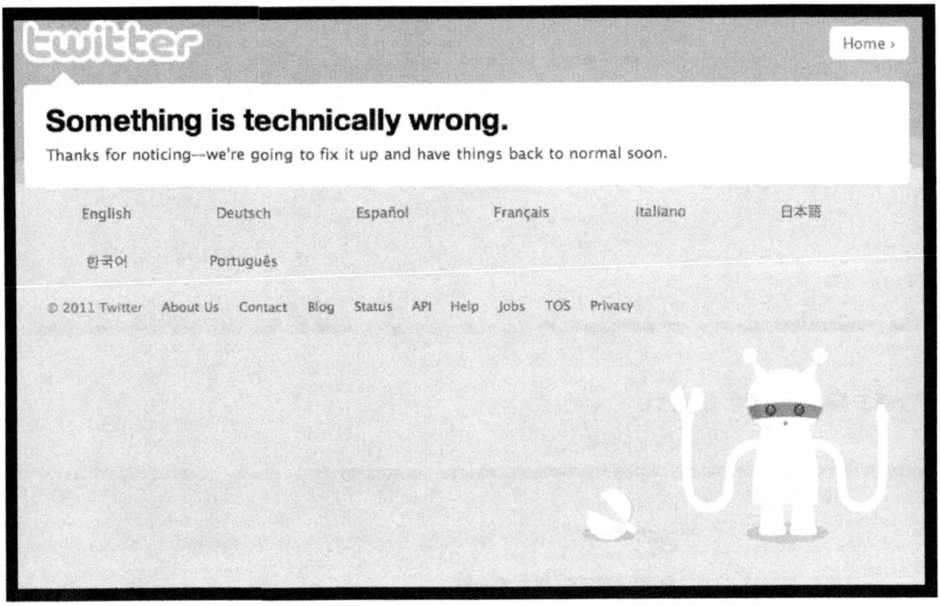

We're Sorry, But Something Went Wrong

Unplanned Maintenance

Chapter 5

Secrets to Getting Followers

THE SECRET TO GETTING ONE+ MILLION FOLLOWERS IN 25 HOURS AND 17 MINUTES.

First you need to be on the #1 sitcom in the country. Then you have to be spectacularly fired, and then kinda implode personally. After that sign onto Twitter and watch those followers accumulate. From signon on March 1 until 25 hours and 17 minutes later on March 2, you'll reach your millionth follower and make the Guinness Book of World Records "Fastest Person to Reach 1 Million Followers on Twitter" record. Charlie Sheen (along with his Tiger blood) shattered the previous record holder Oprah Winfrey who reached one million followers in thirty days.

However, it is unlikely the above scenario applies to you. So, you're going to have a bit harder time of it. But you can get to 100,000+ followers.

First you have to understand how Twitter works. There are some limits to following and unfollowing. Pay attention to these limits. Repeated violation of some of them will get your account suspended.

TWITTER LIMITS

Direct Messages: 250 per day.

Updates (Tweets, Retweets): 1,000 per day, but space them out. And it is not cumulative. If you only use 200 follows one day the other 800 do not accumulate to the next day. Use it or lose it. If anyone knows, let me know.

Changes to Account Email: 4 per hour, though I can't imagine why anyone would need to do that.

Following (daily): Maximum of 1000 daily. But in reality you won't get close to that. You'll probably be able to follow 400-700 a day. And that should be plenty. I have noticed that if you don't tweet you can't follow a whole lot of people. If you tweet a lot you seem to be able to follow more people.

Magic 2000 following: You can follow the first 2000 people without the equivalent number following you back. Once you reach 2000 people you can only follow 10% more than 2000 providing 2000 are following you back. Until that 2200:2000 follower ratio you can't follow anyone else. More on this in a few paragraphs.

Keep Tweeting: You can't just follow and unfollow people without tweeting. You must tweet regularly. If you don't Twitter will notice and your account might be suspended. And the purpose for being on Twitter is to tweet. So, why wouldn't you tweet a lot?

When you hit a limit Twitter will let you know with an error message:

Some limits are time-based (DMs, Updates, Account Email Changes, API Requests). You just have to wait out the time-limit, usually a few hours, to a day.

If you reach the follower limit, technically 1000 maximum, but you'll never get close to that, then you won't be able to follow anyone else until the next day sometime.

Tips for following as many people as possible per day.

Tweet. If you don't tweet you won't be able to follow many people. I've experiment on one account. I didn't tweet for several days and then tried following twitterers. I received the unable to follow message after 100 follows.

WHAT WILL GET YOUR ACCOUNT SUSPENDED?

Aggressive Following and Unfollowing Will Do It

Aggressive following/unfollowing is called churning and is not allowed. Nor do you need to do it. Be patient, follow a few hundred people a day. A few times a week unfollow those who haven't followed you back. Follow intelligently, primarily people of like interest. And tweet. Tweeting and becoming interesting on Twitter will get you more followers than following/unfollowing. But, until you know what to tweet, then following/unfollowing is a way to build up followers.

Using Automated Follow Programs

These types of programs have built in API functions so they don't exceed Twitter's limits. However, if they make a mistake and do exceed those limits your account may be suspended. Be very careful using these types of programs. I don't recommend them because you don't need to use them. I think they're a waste of money.

Insulting Someone

Don't be abrasive. There's no reason to insult other people.

Releasing Someone Else's Personal Information

You cannot post someone else's personal information, such as address, telephone number, anything considered private. Do so and you account will be suspended.

Don't Pretend To Be Someone You're Not

Unless you really are a specific celebrity don't post pretending to be that person. Pretending to be a friend you're angry with and trying to get back at is also verboten. Don't do it. Your Twitter account should be you, or a topic/business you're interested in promoting.

GETTING PAST THAT MAGIC 2000 LIMIT

Your first hurdle is going to be getting past the Magic 2000 followers. You can follow as many people as you want until you reach 2000 followers. Then you can't follow any more people until 2000 people are following you at which point the 10% rule kicks in. You can follow 10% more people than the number who follow you. So once you have 2000 followers you can follow 2000 + 10% overage or 2200 people. And that number will increase as your followers increase.

The 10% rule applies for all future follower:follow ratios. For example if 5000 people are following you then you can follow 5000 plus 10% more or 5500 people. At 10,000 followers you can follow 11,000. There's no way around this limit. Some people have difficulty getting followers and their account pretty much comes to a halt until they get 2000 followers.

If you don't have a quick followback ratio you will find yourself unable to follow anyone once you follow 2000 people until your followers catch up and 2000 people are following you. On average you'll get about 30-50% return followback of most people you follow. That means you'll reach your 2000 limit fairly rapidly and only have about 600-1000 people following you back.

What can you do? You can wait until more people follow you. Or you can unfollow those who don't follow you back. How do you know who isn't following you? How can you delete people efficiently without wasting a lot of time?

http://dossy.org/twitter/karma/

Twitter Karma works great for those who are just starting out. You can easily find those you follow who don't follow you back and unfollow them.

Make certain you are logged into your Twitter account. Then hit the "Sign in with Twitter" OAuth verification button. If you aren't logged into Twitter the screen will ask you to do so. After you're logged in Twitter Karma will have the ability to go through your account and generate data comparing your Followers and Unfollowers.

Here's a helpful suggestion to the creator of this website. Move the "Hide Avatars?" select box above the Whack! button since its a decision you want to make before you hit the Whack! button.

First select the "Hide Avatars?" checkbox. You don't want the website also having to show little profile pictures of each person. Showing avatars will slow things down a lot. And if you have several thousand followers it might take a long time to crawl through your Twitter account.

Twitter Karma is very effective up to about 10,000 followers. However if the page hasn't loaded after five minutes you might have to refresh the page and hit the WHACK! button again, and maybe even once more, for it to crawl through all your entire Twitter account.

Once it does load do a "Sort by: Last Updated" and "Show Only Following". This will show you the people only you are following. They aren't following you back. You can select to just flush them all, or unfollow specific people.

Once your follow numbers are back under 2000 you can start following again. Eventually you'll get past the Magic 2000 followers limit and be able to start following again.

You have to start regularly flushing those who don't follow you.

There are other Twitter management websites (see page 171). Twitter Karma is easy to use and eases you into following/unfollowing. Once you reach 8,000-10,000 followers it becomes impractical to use and you'll have to move onto to something more powerful.

My favorite Twitter management program is Tweepi. This is the Twitter Management website I use. If you want to plunge right in and skip using Twitter Karma you can go to Chapter 6 (see page 145) and learn all about how to use Tweepi.

BUYING FOLLOWERS

You're going to run into a lot of companies that are going to try to sell you followers. Prices vary greatly. However, I do not endorse buying followers. It's a waste of money. Remember your best followers are targeted followers. Or following followers of topics you're interested in.

You don't need to pay to get followers. As I said, it's just a waste of money.

FOLLOW/UNFOLLOW SOFTWARE PROGRAMS

If you're on Twitter any length of time you'll receive an ad for software programs that guarantee to get you followers. Twitter does not sanction these programs. And sometimes using these programs will result in your account being suspended.

Just about the only advantage to some of these programs is that they do have a built-in autoresponder-autowelcome function.

I have tested all these programs. You don't need to spend any money on them. You can very easily do everything they do, and with better results.

So, save your money. Many of the capabilities offered by these programs are now available free online, which makes it convenient to be able to logon to a website and manage your Twitter account without having to be at a specific computer that has software loaded on it.

FOLLOWER WEBSITES

A lot of "Get Followers Quick" websites pop up. Although they bill themselves as "FREE!!", that's only for the limited program. In order to generate a lot of followers you have to join the "PRO" paid program. And the way the price is structured most people go for the Annual Membership. However these websites seldom last a year. In fact some barely last 60 days (past the PayPal refund limit). These types of websites appear very quickly and then after making some money disappear only to reappear doing the same thing under a different name. Sometimes they might even have a dozen sites doing exactly the same thing, with websites that vary only in color schemes. I found over a dozen websites run by one person. I could tell because the websites were identical except for color scheme and he had the same words misspelled in his Terms of Service. Usually the TOS says there are no refunds for any reason. However, if you find yourself scammed email the website and tell them you're going to have PayPal do a full investigation of their practices over every account they use on PayPal. They will be only too happy make an exception to their no refund rule.

If the scammer is running the same website under different names and you logon to one, they use your name on the others, too because they need to show how many members they have. They don't have a whole lot of members on each website, so combine them to get to about 4,000-6,000 members.

These scam websites proliferate very quickly and get lots of signups in a few weeks. That's because when someone signs up for a Free account they have to give the website permission to Tweet ads about their website on the user's twitterstream and send updates about how many followers you're gaining using their service.

Another indicator is that they usually have the word follow in their URL: getfollowersfast.com, fastfollowers.com, etc. Both those URLs at one point promised you fast followers. They lasted a very short time.

These scam websites also might have the word "train" in them as in "Join our Twitter Train and get massive numbers of followers." Please, don't get on the train. You'll regret it because the train will take all your money and won't stop to let you off. You'll have to jump out a window to get off that train. You're going to get hurt.

These programs promise you the moon in followers. Tens of thousands of followers. But, if they're on Twitter at all look at how many followers they have. Usually just a few thousand. If their program worked they'd have tens of thousands of followers, wouldn't they?

And they also will tout that they have thousands of members, usually about 4,000-6,000, a number which includes both free and paid Pro accounts. Think about it logically. All of your follows are coming from their members of which you are one. If they have only 6,000 members how can they get you tens of thousands of followers? Doesn't make sense. This is why their website hangs around for a few weeks/months and then disappears, usually resurfacing under a different name promising even greater numbers of followers.

Avoid websites with the word "train", "followback", "getfollowersfast" or similar terms, in their URL. These websites violate Twitter's Terms of Service and you might find your account suspended. How does Twitter know you're using one of these websites? Because of all the complains about you for the spam the website is doing through your twitterstream (remember you gave them access to your Twitter account when you signed up).

And for another thing, they just don't work. You're wasting your money and risking getting your Twitter account suspended for nothing. Don't do that.

Twiends (http://twiends.com)

The only website I've seen and tried that actually works at building followers through following on their website is Twiends. You can build up points by following others, and then offer people points for following you. Some people will offer nine points, others one, and some zero. I'd say try two points maximum.

Build up your points by following others and also by watching Youtube videos. People will award you various amounts of points (up to 9) for watching their videos. You don't have to watch the entire video. If they're offering one or two points you only have to watch maybe twenty seconds. If they're offering nine points you may have to watch 90 second. So, you can always have two computers on and "watch" videos while you're working on your other computer. Look up occasionally and click on the video after you've watched it to take you back to the list of other videos to watch. A lot of the members do run the same video, but even if you've seen it before, you still get points for watching it. Just by passively watching and following people you can probably build up enough points to get a hundred or so followers per day. However, one caveat. I've found that a huge number of the people who follow you from Twiends, unfollow in a few days, I guess, hoping you won't notice they've unfollowed you. But, you will if you follow our Twitter management suggestions (see page 145).

You can buy Twiend points, but you don't really need to. Just follow to get points, and watch YouTube videos to get points.

YOU SHOULD UNDER NO CIRCUMSTANCES FOLLOW THESE PEOPLE

Let's start with the people you shouldn't follow. This will get rid of a big chunk of people for you.

Spammers

Spammers are the lowest of the low. Generally the people who follow spammers will follow anyone. So they are the low hanging fruit if you want a bunch of quick followers. But, I don't really want followers like that. They tend to get bored with Twitter and leave. Waste of time following them to just get them to follow you back. Low percentages overall.

And a word of warning. Don't follow a spammer, That gives them your name so they know in the future you might be a mark. Or your followers might be a mark.

Can spammers actually make money on Twitter. Yes indeed, and they do it by volume spamming. Some spammers might open a hundred Twitter accounts a day and follow 2000 on each account. Remember they can follow up to 2000 without having to have 2000 people follow them back. At that point the 10% overage rule kicks in. But, they don't care. The account is going to be closed in a day or two by the spammer or by Twitter.

Their products are usually get rich quick schemes, diet/weight loss schemes, acai berry miracle schemes, veeagra herbal supplements schemes. If someone tells you they made $100,000 on the internet last month, run from them. They made money from people who believed they made $100,000 on the internet last month. They're lying. The screen shots they show you are PhotoShopped. The "live" videos they show you, aren't.

Let's look at the financials of spamming. Those 100 accounts equals 200,000 people. If they get just 1% to click on their link (2,000) and .5% of those to buy something, that's 10 sales a day. Their products are usually priced between $50-$100 initially. So that's $500-$1000 per day. But when the person agrees to buy the product usually there's a hidden permission that let's them charge the person's credit card every month. And they're hoping like most people the person doesn't check their credit card statement that regularly. So, for the spammer this is all well worth the hassle of spamming.

Oh, wait what hassle? How do they open so many accounts and follow so many people? It's all automated with computer software programs. And, of course, they don't actually have to deliver the product. Or, they might just give a link to a one page summary of something.

Soon after they open their account Twitter starts receiving lots of complaints and shuts them down. Doesn't matter to the spammer because they're onto creating other accounts.

Signs Someone Is a Spammer:

- They frequently take celebrity names and put either fan, is awesome, or numbers [123] after the celebrities' name. But their tweets don't have anything to do with the celebrity. Usually their tweets lead to a squeeze page selling you some quick rich scheme or health product.
- Their profile picture is the default egg. They know this twitterstream isn't going to last long, so why bother customizing it?
- The background image is either the default, or they've used one of Twitter's default background.
- Their bio information is sparse and sometimes outlandishly made up.

CELEBRITIES, ONE-PERSON WONDERS

You don't want to follow people who are devoted to one person. For the most part it's not good to follow celebrities or their followers. The celebrity isn't going to follow you back and their followers are only interested in the celebrity and are not interested in you or anyone else.

For example, teenage girls following Justin Bieber, or Miley Cyrus don't do much else on Twitter. They don't followback. They aren't interested. At some point they may outgrow their infatuation and become more interested in the overall Twitter community. But, until then, don't bother following them.

FOCUSSED BUSINESSES

Focussed businesses are companies who sell a product that appeals to very few people. Their followers generally are only interested in that product. Unless your twitterstream is about that product their followers are not going to be interested in you or what you have to say. It's a waste of time following them.

FOLLOWING AND UNFOLLOWING

Unless you're really famous, the only way to get followers is to followback (as well as being incredibly interesting posting fascinating tweets). It's considered a courtesy to do so. Some people will follow you to get you to followback. And then in a few days they'll unfollow you thinking you won't notice. But, you will notice and unfollow them. You can find further information about managing your Twitter account later in this book (see pages 145 and 171).

You have to unfollow those who unfollow you. Remember you only have a 10% overage of people whom you can follow. So, unless you are particularly interested in their tweets don't waste one of your follows. You can always search them and read their tweets. But, you can't interact if you both don't follow each other. Likewise if you don't followback then that person can't DM you and will probably unfollow you.

WHOM TO FOLLOW

Community

Twitter is a community about making connections and being interested in what other people have to say. In order for that to happen you'll follow people who interest you and others will follow you. And sometimes you'll have to unfollow people because of Twitter's limits that you can only follow 10% more than the number of people who follow you.

Should you follow everyone who follows you? Yes, it's common courtesy. There is one proviso and that's if their views of life are reprehensible to you. Then you not only shouldn't follow them you should block them if they're following you. And if someone follows you and then unfollows you, then you should unfollow them.

The only way people can DM you (send a private Direct Message) is if you both mutually follow each other. That's the best reason to follow everyone who follows you. That way you can engage in private conversation with someone. Otherwise if they tweet you with a question it shows up on both your twitterstreams. And it might be something personal they'd rather ask you privately.

Follow:

- People interested in what you are interested in. They will then retweet you and you'll get more followers
- Follow people in your industry/professions
- Follow people you know
- Follow interesting people

Don't Get Frustrated

Some days on Twitter no matter what you do, your followers just won't increase much. Very few people seem to be following you back. Just realize it's just one of those days. I've found Saturdays to be brutal. Just give up and go to a movie. I had one day when I refreshed and had suddenly LOST 50 followers. I eventually gained more. But, it can be disheartening. Don't worry about it. Overall, you're going to have an upward trend.

There is the flip side. Other days there's a swarm of people following you back.

Just be prepared for days when nothing happens, and days when you go through the roof.

Avoid the temptation to every few seconds hit the refresh button on your browser to see how many more people have followed you because it's going to fluctuate, and sometimes wildly. You'll like it when you hit refresh and find your followers have gone up by 30. Then you hit refresh again and you've lost 10. Hit it again and you've lost 25. That means you're down -5 from before. Then you hit it again and you're up 20. Then up 50, then down 20.

If you keep hitting refresh and watching your followers increase and decrease you'll go crazy. At first its easy to see why your followers increase. People can see you're interesting because of your tweets. But then when you lose followers, what can that be about? First time it happens you'll think "Why don't they like me?"

It's not you. People unfollow for many reasons. They might have hit the Magic 2000 limit and need to unfollow people. Maybe they've been suspended? Or decided to close their account? So, don't sweat it. At the end of the day you'll have more followers than when you started. Doesn't matter how it fluctuated throughout the day. So, if you have enough willpower just refresh your Twitter page a couple of times a day. Of course, I am not blessed with such patience and refresh a lot more than a few times a day. And I see the fluctuations which is why I'm warning you about it. Doesn't matter. And it's not personal unless someone sends you a tweet telling you why they've unfollowed you.

Targeted Followers

Targeted Followers = Targeted Traffic

Targeted followers are the crème de la crème of followers. They're interested in what you're interested in. They're following you because they want to read what you have to tweet. They aren't just following you to have you followback. A thousand targeted followers are much better than 10,000 scattershot untargeted followers.

However, I do understand that sometimes it's about numbers and building a presence on Twitter in which case you want as many followers as you can get. But if you're going to sell something, or try to influence people, the ones who will respond will be your targeted followers. Hopefully, after reading your tweets for a while some of those untargeted followers will discover they actually agree with you/want to read your tweets/want to buy what you're selling. At that point they've become targeted followers.

Finding Targeted Followers:

Unless you're mass following to build up an audience you might want to be picky. So, how do you decide whom to follow?

Look at what they post:

- Are they interesting?
- Are they tweeting about things you're interested in?
- Are they thought-provoking?
- Are they useful, amusing, entertaining?
- Is it about "me me me", or are they helpful to others?
- Do you like what they tweet?
- Is it similar to what you tweet?
- Can you see yourself retweeting their tweets?
- Do you follow a lot of people they follow?
- Do a lot of their followers also follow you?

Answering yes to many of the above shows common interests or a common client base if you are a business.

Another way to find targeted followers is to look at the tweets in your twitterstream. If you find some interesting tweets click on the [twitter_id] of the person who tweeted and read their older tweets. If you like what you read, then follow them. There's a good chance they'll check you out and followback.

HOW TO GET PEOPLE TO FOLLOW YOU

After you've opened your Twitter account only follow people you actually know. They'll hopefully follow you back.

Then begin tweeting. Don't try to get followers for several weeks. Build up a hundred tweets or so. Make them interesting and useful. "Going to the grocery store." "Going out tonight." "Going shopping" "Going to a movie." Those kinds of tweets just don't cut it for building up a following. It's okay for friends to read, but, seriously, who else is going to be the least bit interested?

Reply to anyone who asks you a question or comments about one of your tweets. Even if it's only to tell them thank you.

If someone retweets you then tweet them a thank you. Follow them and try to find something of theirs to retweet.

Start retweeting interesting tweets in your twitterstream.

Comment on other people's tweets, but only if your comment is complimentary. Don't engage in arguments. Don't trespass onto someone else's account and criticize them. Follow Thumper's father's advice (most people think it's Thumper's mother's advice but she asks him to remember what Thumper's father told him that morning):

> "If you can't say something nice, don't say nothing at all."

You're just starting out on Twitter. You don't want to begin as a person who isn't very nice. As I keep emphasizing it's all about community and interaction. You don't want to be the bad neighbor everyone avoids.

Don't even try to get followers until you've gotten the hang of tweeting. Learn how to send links with link shorteners (see pages 89 and 167). Learn how to upload photos (see page 90). After a few weeks you'll have settled down into some topics you want to tweet about. You'll be following some interesting people. You'll be retweeting. You'll be engaging in conversation. At that point you're ready to start getting followers.

Most people on Twitter are not going to go over the 2000 limit. They aren't interested in getting lots of followers. They are interested in following interesting people and learning things. That's why you have to be serious about what you tweet. People just aren't going to follow you if your tweets are mundane, uninteresting, or boring.

And you have to tweet often, otherwise people just think you're a stale account. But, don't tweet too often. Just because you can send a thousand tweets a day doesn't mean you have to send a thousand tweets a day. You have to send enough tweets every day to be interesting enough to attract people, and to be retweeted. Being retweeted is an excellent way to expand your audience.

The more people who follow you on Twitter, the more influence and networking opportunities you have. Thus, it makes sense to try and build a following. To summarize here are some rules for getting people to follow you:

- Follow other twitterers. There's an almost kneejerk reaction to follow people who follow you. However, there's a backlash against people who follow just about everyone for the sole purpose of gaining followers. In short, be discriminating with whom you follow.
- Post some good tweets right before following someone else. Would you want to follow someone who only tweets about how hungry or tired they are; or they're bored and can't think of anything to do or say (why tweet then?); or why on earth would someone want to see that movie? The same goes for people who

haven't tweeted in a while. Do you want to follow someone with only one or two tweets three months ago after they signed on?

- Complete your bio. People rarely follow strangers, so complete your one-line bio and include a URL in the More Info URL section of your profile.
- Add your Twitter feed to your blog or to other social media profiles. If you have a following on your blog or a lot of connections at facebook or LinkedIn, you can leverage this audience to increase your followers at Twitter.
- Reply to people you are following, especially if they're not yet following you. That's a good way to engage someone and get them to follow you, even if they didn't follow you immediately. Remember, though, some people have thousands of followers, and may not be able to respond to every reply.
- Be helpful to people on Twitter and they will follow you. Give them use information and they will follow you.

FOLLOW FRIDAY

Every Friday twitterers will suggested followers to other twitterers using the #FF hashtag (see page 79 for more about hashtags). Some will use #FollowFriday but that takes up a lot of characters and people know #FF means Follow Friday. It's great to be included in someone's Follow Friday list. You should create your own #FF each Friday and tweet it. This shows you are part of the community. And it's nice to let others know about people you like on Twitter.

CREATE YOUR NICHE

Create your own niche on Twitter. Tweet about a topic, a hobby, something of interest to you. Make yourself unique in your niche on Twitter. Become an authority. Give people some reason to check your tweets.

You might not think you're an authority on anything. But everyone's an authority on something. What special skills do you have? Maybe you're the world's best housekeeper. That's valuable. Being able to tweet how to efficiently clean your house so you don't have to take a lot of time doing it could be an extremely useful twitterstream.

Maybe you tie the best fishing lures in the world. Become the Twitter expert on fishing lures (linking to photos and instructions, even instructional videos on YouTube (become a YouTube partner and you'll get paid through google adsense).

There's at least one thing you're truly great at. Build a Twitter account around that niche. (And remember you can have more than one Twitter account.)

Niche accounts are the easiest type of Twitter account to get followers. You might not get a lot of followers, but those you do get are golden. They're targeted to your niche. They're interested in your tweets because they're interested in the topic, or have the same hobby.

You might want to have a general Twitter account with lots of followers, and then niche accounts for targeted followers. I have my general Twitter account, and a niche account aimed at graphic design/web design/photography. It only has about 19,000 followers, but they're targeted followers and more likely to listen to what I say, retweet me, or buy something I recommend.

How Do You Find Niche Followers?

Niche followers are amongst the easiest to find and easiest to interest in following you back.

Go to "Find People" in the menu. Just because the menu item is titled "Find People" you can search for topics, too because the end result is a list of twitterers.

Type in the niche area(s) of interest for your twitterstream. Up will pop a list of people who have expressed interest in that topic or hobby. Start following them. They'll check you out first, but if they see by the name on your account, or your tweets, that you're tweeting about things they're interested in, they'll follow you.

Because of twitter's limited search engine you may find only a few hundred people when there are actually a few thousand. Twitter management and finding people to follow is discussed later in this book (see pages 145 and 171).

SEARCHING FOR FOLLOWERS

Two types of Searches: Targeted, Non-Specific

I've already discussed the advantages of finding targeted followers. There won't be as many as in a general search, but those you find are golden.

If you're interested in building a huge following then non-specific is the way to go.

Non-specific followers tend to be generalists, and have lots of interests and seem to be following diverse people.

Twitterers who have high followback rates include marketing people, salespeople, and SEO (Search Engine Optimization) people. Their high followback rate is because these are people who are interested in networking and finding others to follow. Follow their followers, too, since they also tend to be in marketing, sales, or SEO, and have a high followback rate.

Searching Using Twitter's Search Function

There are two ways to search on Twitter. The first is from the "Find People" menu which I've discussed.

The second will give you a far better search. This is a search using http://search.twitter.com.

Searching Screen

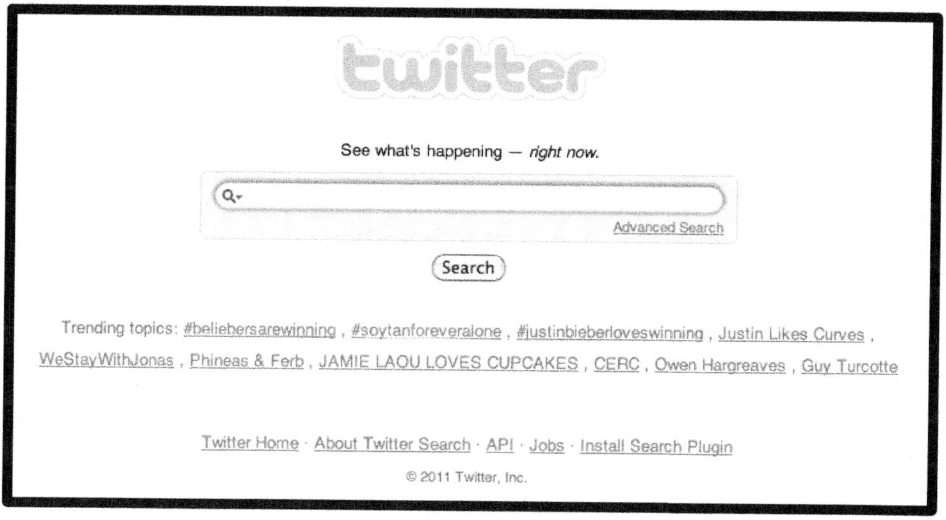

Notice that there's a "Trending topics" section under the search field. You can just click on a Trending topic to search it without having to input it in the search field.

Also notice the "Install Search Plugin" on the lower right. This puts a plugin on your menu bar, but only for certain browsers: IE, Firefox, Aurora, and Google Chrome.

You should search for your own [twitter_id]. This will yield your recent tweets, people who have replied to your tweets, people who have retweeted you, and people who have commented about you. If you've missed someone's reply or comment you can reply to it here.

Once you do a search for your [twitter_id] you can drag that search URL to your menu bar. Then the next time you want to search, just click on the menu bar icon and it'll bring up the latest search about you. The search URL will be http://search.twitter.com/search?q=[twitter_id].

This Twitter search is still limited. However notice the "Advanced Search" under the Search field. If you click on that you'll get a page of expanded options:

This boosts Twitter's search capabilities into something really useful. You can set criteria for Word, People, Places, Dates, Attitudes (positive, negative, questioning attitude), and other criteria including links and retweets. You can list up to 50 results per page. Using this expanded criteria you can really target your searches.

Things to Search for:

Search for Hot Topics to find topics people are talking about that aren't in Trending Topics. The results can give you some interesting, popular things to tweet about.

Here are some topics to search for with high followback percentages:

- SEO
- eMarketing
- eCommerce
- sales
- real estate
- how to get followers
- follow4follow
- followback
- I followback

Yes, searching for "how to get followers, follow4follow, followback, I followback" will get you names of people who are trying to get followers. Look at their profiles and if they have several thousand, they're succeeding and their followers probably have a high followback percentage

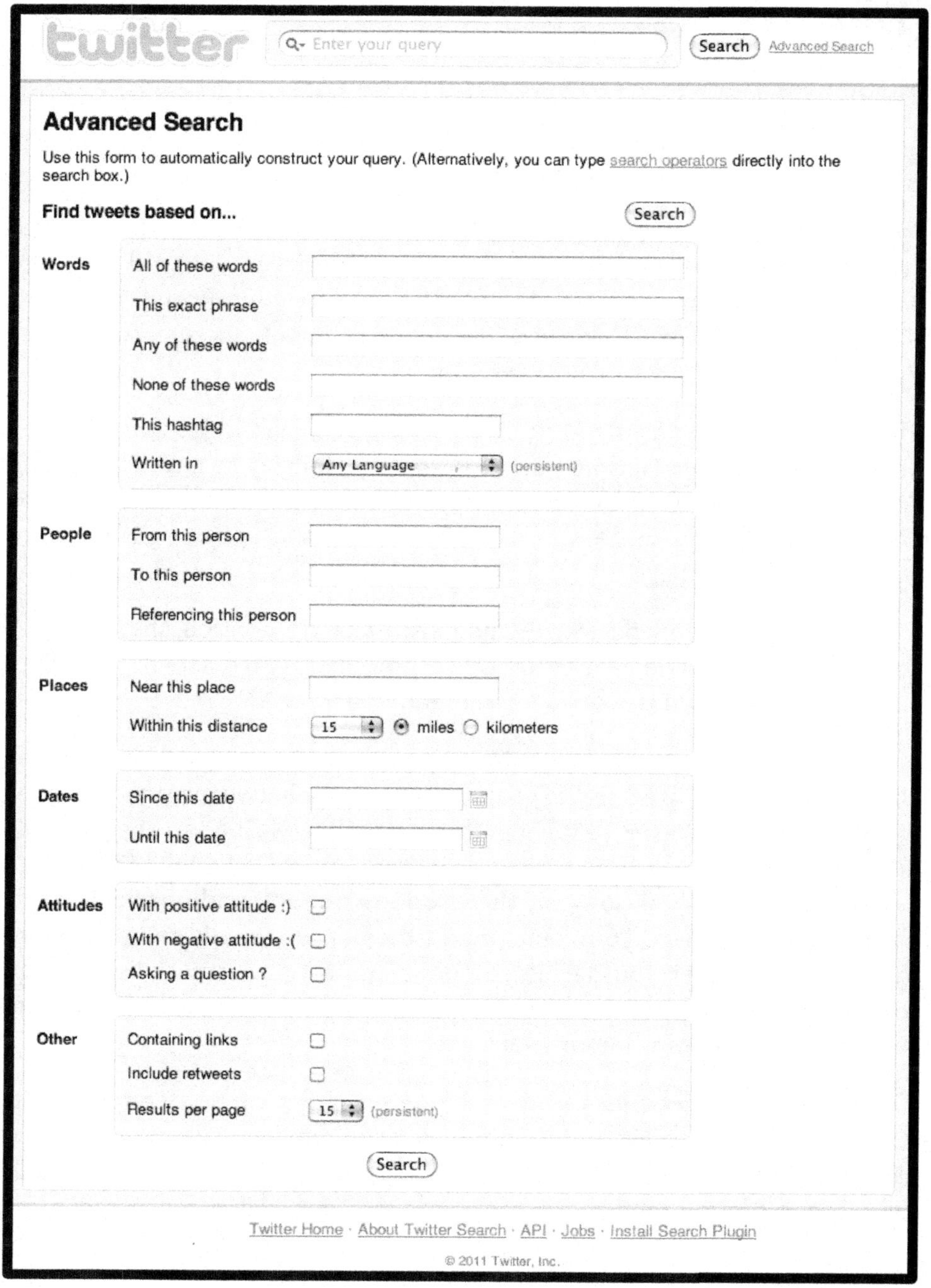

twitter | Enter your query | Search | Advanced Search

Advanced Search

Use this form to automatically construct your query. (Alternatively, you can type search operators directly into the search box.)

Find tweets based on... Search

Words
- All of these words
- This exact phrase
- Any of these words
- None of these words
- This hashtag
- Written in: Any Language (persistent)

People
- From this person
- To this person
- Referencing this person

Places
- Near this place
- Within this distance: 15 miles / kilometers

Dates
- Since this date
- Until this date

Attitudes
- With positive attitude :)
- With negative attitude :(
- Asking a question ?

Other
- Containing links
- Include retweets
- Results per page: 15 (persistent)

Search

Twitter Home · About Twitter Search · API · Jobs · Install Search Plugin

© 2011 Twitter, Inc.

LISTS AND LISTORIOUS.COM

Another great way to get followers is through Lists.

Creating Your Own Lists

You should be creating your own lists on Twitter. It's easy to do. Login to Twitter and go to your Profile page (if you're already logged in go to twitter.com/[twitter_id]. This should take you to your Profile page. You should see the words "That's you!" under your Profile picture. And to the right should be a "Lists" drop down menu.

There are two reasons if you don't see this. You aren't logged into Twitter, or you are on your "Home" page. If you are logged in and don't see a Profile picture, but see "What's happening?" above a tweet field, then you are on your "Home" page. Click on "Profile" in the upper right menu to get to your Profile page.

Click on the Lists dropdown menu. If you haven't created any lists then you'll see "New list". If you've created some lists, you'll see all your lists, and at the bottom of the dropdown menu you'll see "New list".

Make as many lists as you want. When you're reading through Twitter and click on someone's [twitter_id] to take you to their twitterpage you'll see whether or not you're following them on the left under their Profile picture. And on the right is a Lists dropdown menu. You can add them to one of your lists by clicking on the dropdown menu and checking a box next to the list where you want to add them. You can add them to more than one list. If, later, you decide you don't want them on that list, then go to their Profile page, click on the list dropdown menu and uncheck them to remove them from one or more lists.

The great thing about lists is that if you see a list on someone's profile you can click on that list and then follow people individually on the list, or click the "Follow this list" button at the top of the list and automatically follow everyone on the list.

You want to be listed by others because people go to lists and then follow everyone on that list. That means you'll get a lot of followers from being listed. You really have no control over who lists you. But you can see how many lists you're on by looking in your sidebar. Next to the "following", "followers" fields is the "listed" field and the number of lists you're listed in. Click on "listed"and all the lists you're listed on shows up in the main part of your page.

How Do You Find Lists?

The "Fine People" menu option in Twitter does not do list searches. However, you're not out of luck. There's a website called Listorious.com. Once you're at their opening page click on the "Search" button and you'll be taken to their main page. Here you can sign in using Twitter's OAuth validation.

You can search for people, or lists. If you want to find people who will follow you back do a search for "follow4follow" or "followback". What you'll get are lists of people who promise to followback anyone who follows them. Although I've found an amazing number of these people don't actually followback and I find myself having to unfollow them.

Click on the list you're interested in. The twitterers on the list will show up and you can follow them individually. But, if you click on "View on Twitter" the list opens up on Twitter with the "Follow this list" button so you can follow everyone all at once.

Click on the "Tags" menu in the upper right menu bar and you'll get a list of the Top Tags on Listorious. Look at the subjects you're interest in to find people who are also interested in those subjects.

You can also find lists of topics you're interested in and which you feature in your tweets. These twitterers should have a high followback percentage because they would be interested in what you're interested in.

You can also list your lists on listorious.com. That way people can find you and those whom you recommend through your list.

Be certain to join Listorious and fill out their survey. You'll get some followers from this site on a regular basis, even if you don't use it again. If you use Listorious you should be able to find lots of targeted followers.

AUTORESPONDER/AUTOWELCOME MESSAGES

Many people send follow-up messages to those who follow them. These are called autoresponder or autowelcome messages. There used to be a lot of free online autoresponder services that would automatically send a message right after someone followed you. But now they charge. You can, of course, send a message manually, or use a paid service. Twitter allows you 250 DM's per day.

If you're going to use an autoresponder make certain your message is friendly and generic. If you're too specific the message might be inappropriate or confusing to the person who followed. Not everyone realizes someone is sendng an autowelcome message and might be puzzled why you're thanking them.

I personally don't send autoresponders because I receive more than 250 followers per day and would use up my DM allotment. I generally use my DM's to respond to people who contact me with questions or comments. A lot of people pay no attention to autoresponder messages so you're wasting your 250 DMs.

HOW TO TELL IF SOMEONE IS FOLLOWING YOU

If you use a Twitter management website like Tweepi (see page 145) then they'll give you a list of those who are following you whom you aren't following, and those you're following who aren't following you.

Not Following

However, you can also tell just by looking at their account. If you aren't following them you'll see the follow button under their profile picture. If you click on the dropdown menu next to the lists menu you'll see the option to follow the person. And in the right sidebar under Actions there's no option to "message" the person.

For example, Charlie Sheen doesn't follow me (your loss Charlie), so I don't follow him (would if he would – your move Charlie).

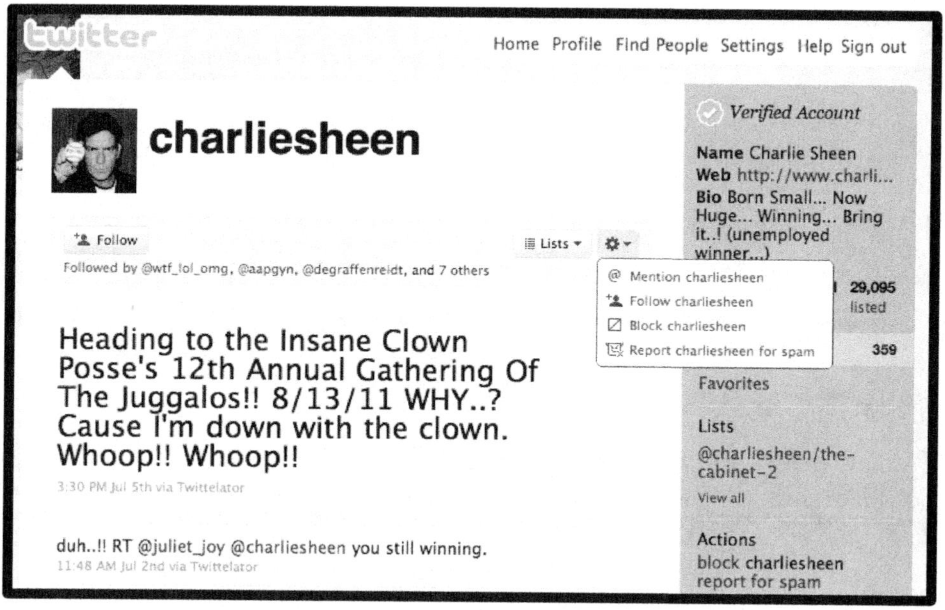

Following

If you are following someone you'll see a checkmark in front of the Following button under their profile picture. If you click on the dropdown menu next to the lists menu you'll see the option to unfollow the person. And in the right sidebar under Actions there's an option to "message" the person. BTW follow ElinorLipman and read her books. Wonderful writer.

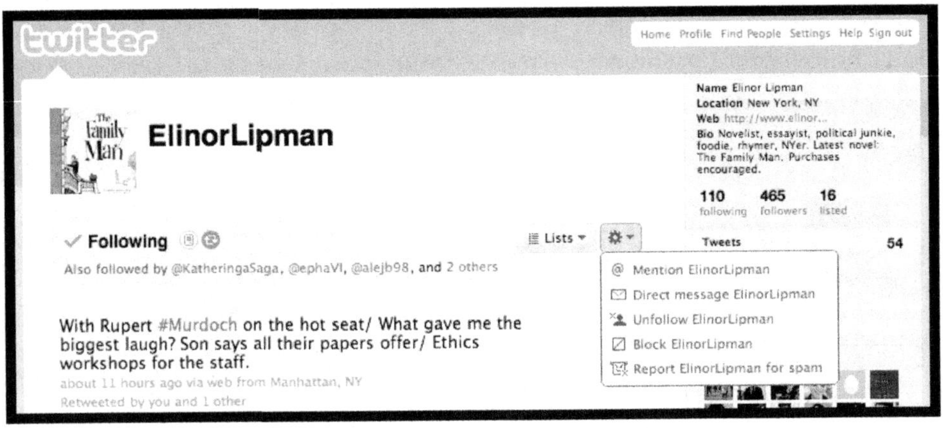

Favoriting, Replying, Retweeting

Twitter gives you an option of favoriting a tweet (comparable to bookmarking a URL). When you hover your cursor over a tweet a star

appears on the right side of that tweet. If you click on the star it turns yellow and remains visible when you move your cursor away from the

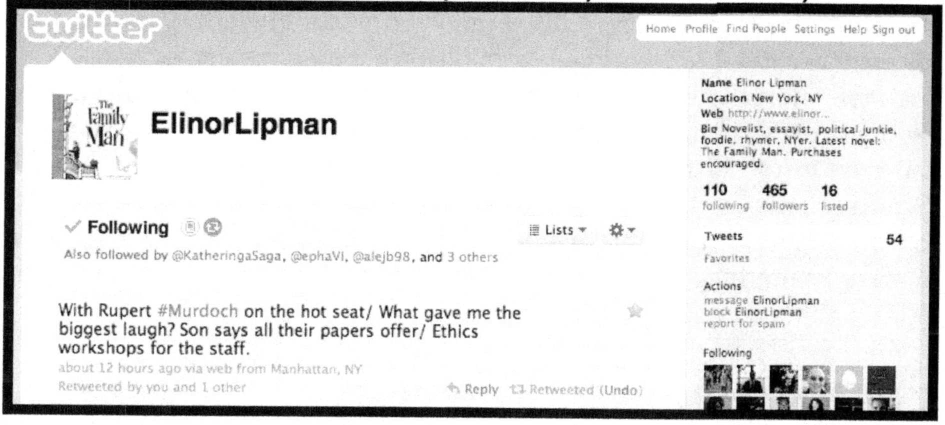

tweet. You have just favorited that tweet. If you've favorited a tweet and want to change your mind just click on the yellow star to unfavorite/ deselect it.

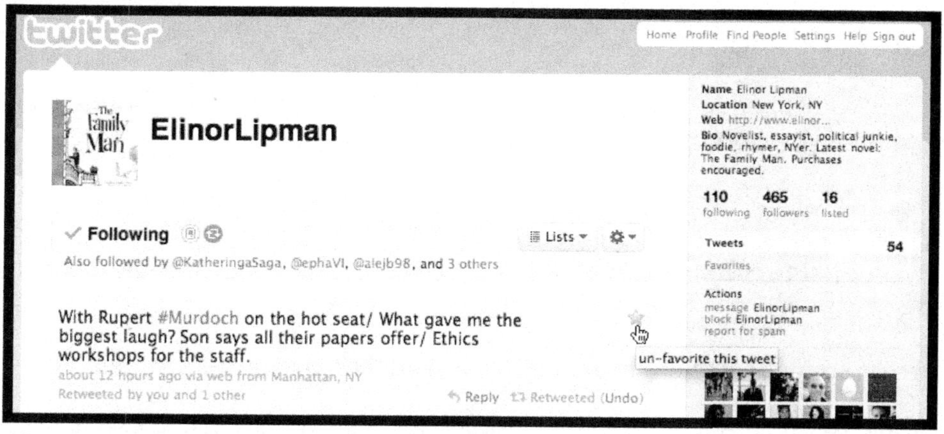

Also when you hover over a person's tweet you'll see the words "Reply" and "Retweet" under the star. You can reply to the twitterer if you want. If you just hit reply the reply will be public and appears in both your twitterstreams. So if it's something personal you might want to DM (Direct Message) the person (see page 204). You cannot favorite your own tweet since you can just look back through your twitterstream to find the tweet. However, if you hover your cursor over one of your own tweets a trash can and the word "delete" appears under the star giving you the option of deleting that tweet. If you want to see a list of your favorited tweets go to this URL: http://Twitter.com/[userID]/favorites, i.e. for my favorites I would input: http://Twitter.com/yvettegr/favorites. One trick for finding followers is to favorite someone in your follow/unfollow twitterstream. Then when you want to follow more of their followers you can type in the http://Twitter.com/[userID]/favorites URL to get to your favorites. That way you don't have to keep a list of those you are following/unfollowing (although it's always a good idea to also keep a list in case something happens and Twitter accidentally has a glitch and deletes all those you've favorited.

THE UNTHINKABLE HAPPENS AND SOMEONE UNFOLLOWS YOU

When you first start getting followers you'll find yourself on your page a lot, refreshing your browser just to see those follower numbers going up and up and up. Until . . .

It has to happen at some point. You're keeping careful track of everything and then you notice it. Someone has unfollowed you. Gasp!

You think, "They've unfollowed me. They've actually unfollowed me! ME! Why? What did I do? Weren't my tweets interesting enough? Something I tweeted? Maybe I should have bought them cake? Don't they love me anymore?" You're a jumble of confused emotions.

Yes, at some point people will unfollow you. And maybe a lot of people.

Don't sweat it. It happens. Most times it's just impersonal. Don't take it personally when someone follows/unfollows you or when your followers go up or down when you check your Twitter account. It doesn't mean they don't like you. Sometimes you just gain or lose a lot of followers for no particular reason.

Sometimes you'll lose followers for bizarre reasons. Once I lost over 100 followers in a few minutes. Why? Because I quoted a medical news article that used the word "penis" in the headline. The linked article was in no was salacious. You'd have thought I'd tweeted about murdering and eating babies. I received DM after DM (before they unfollowed and couldn't DM me any more) telling me there was no place on Twitter for language like that so they were unfollowing. And it was pretty equally divided between men and women. So, when you're unfollowed just think it's probably for something really innocuous. Don't sweat it. You'll have more followers at the end of the day than when you started that morning. and those who unfollowed you so easily would have unfollowed you eventually anyway.

My advice, don't keep refreshing your page to see how many people are following you. You'll find that it goes up and down, and sometimes rather drastically. Do it every hour or so and usually it'll be an upward trend and you won't see the ups and downs that came before.

BEING BLOCKED

There is something worse than being unfollowed, and that is being blocked. Being blocked means you can't follow them at all. They've blocked you. But how? How did they know you were going to follow them?

They might have actually seen your posts and blocked you. Or maybe someone has a block list you're on and the person has just followed / blocked everyone on that list? Being blocked by someone isn't necessarily personal. I've found myself blocked and noticed that the person is probably blocking just about everyone. Some people just don't want to be bothered/followed by anyone. I have no idea why they would be on Twitter.

Again don't sweat it. Some people block everyone automatically don't take it personally. There are hundreds of millions of people on Twitter. At some point one or two of those people won't like you and will block you. Nothing to be concerned about.

Now if thousands of people block you Twitter will take notice and probably suspend your account. People block others because they think they're spammers, or post offensive things. So, don't spam, don't post offensive things. Play nice.

UNKIND MESSAGES FROM THE TROLL UNDER THE BRIDGE (DON'T FEED THE TROLLS)

Sometimes you might feel it necessary to block someone. Don't even hesitate and think that you'll hurt their feelings. Twitter isn't always warm and fuzzy. Sometimes someone you don't even know will take against you and send you unkind and unwanted messages. Ignore them. Don't respond. If that makes them angrier and they persist then block them. If they're very extreme and you recognize that they've created another account after being blocked and are again sending you unkind messages then report them (and messages under their previous identity) to twitter, informing Twitter that you're being abused (because you are). No one should feel unsafe on Twitter. And messages that keep escalating, and someone who creates another account after being blocked and gets even more threatening, needs to be reported to Twitter. Though nothing is ever deleted from Twitter, and they keep EVERYTHING (even after you've deleted something), it's a good idea to keep copies of the tweets. Take a screen shot, and also select and copy them into a text program since that makes it easier to send copies to Twitter. Click on a tweet to bring up it's html page and save that.

Don't let anyone threaten on Twitter (or anywhere else). Report them.

FOLLOW SOMEONE AND FOLLOW THEIR FOLLOWERS

Following someone's followers is the Birds of a Feather theory. If you're following someone because you like their tweets and generally agree with them, then you'll probably like their followers, and their followers will probably like you (follow you) back. I'll concentrate on someone who follows others. Someone who preferably follows everyone who follows them, and perhaps a little more.

I try to concentrate on people of like interests to me (see page 126, Searching for Followers about how to do that). I'll search under certain categories and check out who pops up. If their tweets are interesting and we seem to be tweeting about the same interests then I'll follow them.

And I'll check to see if I should follow their followers, since there's a high probability those people might be interested in what I'm tweeting.

I'll start going through their follower list and see if we have any followers in common. If it seems like we have a lot in common (5-8 common followers per page), I might start following their followers. I have a lot of followers so it's not unusual I'll find a lot of people who follow me also following someone else. If you don't have a lot of followers then you might only find 1 or 2 every page or so. But that's enough to show it might be worthwhile to follow this person's followers. Keep track over a few days of how many follow you back. If a lot from that person's followers follow you back, then it's an indication you should follow more of their followers.

If they do have the same interests as you you'll have a high followback percentage. I do keep track of followback percentages for a twitterer if I'm following their followers. I'll give their followers a few days to follow you back. I don't check followers individually. Just every few days, maybe once a week, I'll log onto Tweepi, go to the last page of those who haven't followed me back and delete several hundred. That way I'm getting rid of people who've had a week or so to follow me back and haven't. You have to unfollow people who don't followback because you have to be concerned with Twitter's 10% over follow percentage. More on how to figure out follower rate and how to unfollow later in this book (see page 145).

When I'm following a twitterer's followers I'll usually go about 100 pages deep. After that everything seems to get a little stale and I notice a sharp fall in the percentage of people who followback. The exception is if after 100 pages I notice there are still a lot of mutual followers on each page, I'll continue following their followers until they start to drops off.

You want fresh followers. The further back you go in their pages the more likely the people aren't tweeting any more or have gotten bored with Twitter but haven't closed their account. I discuss managing following/unfollowing twitterers later in this book (see page 145).

However, if you do choose to follow all their followers and they have a lot, then you're going to go hundreds of pages deep. Pages are not listed as page1, page2, page3, etc. Twitter used to do this, so when you left off at a page you just went to that [twitter_id] and then to the page you left off. But Twitter changed this in September 2009, so that each page is given a unique identifier which shows up at the end of the URL for that page. Just copy the URL where you stopped following and when you want to go back to start following again from the page you left off, even if it's hundreds of pages deep, just paste the URL in you browser and you'll be where you left off.

If the twitterer whose followers I'm following has a good followback percentage then I'll check in on their followers every few days and follow their latest followers. After a while you'll build up a list of twitters who have a high followback percentage and will regularly follow their latest followers.

This list of twitterers will probably yield you more than half of those who follow you back.

KEEPING TRACK OF YOUR FOLLOWING/UNFOLLOWING

If you're going to do following/unfollowing seriously you have to keep track of what you're doing. The simplest way is to use a Microsoft Word document. If you don't have Microsoft Word then go to Openoffice.org and download their free software. 100% compatible with Microsoft Word. Also, you can go to docs.google.com and keep your data online (you'll have to open a gmail account if you don't already have one). In addition to Word you can also make a Spreadsheet to analyze your statistics. (If you subscribe to the yearly subscription I'm offering there will be several free downloadable Word and Spreadsheet templates specifically designed for keeping track of your following/unfollowing (see page xvii).

At the minimum you want to keep track of the following:

| Data | Time | Followers | #Followed Today | #Followed Back Yesterday |

You'll only have a few entries every day.

Followback Strategy

Although you can follow 1000 twitterers per day, don't follow more than 150-200 each time you follow. And only follow 600-700 a day. Don't get greedy. Pigs get fat, hogs get slaughtered.

If you've tweeted a lot the day before then follow 200 per hour. If you haven't tweeted that much then only follow 150 per hour.

Spread out the hours. Don't try to bunch all your follow for a few hours in the morning to get it over with. Twitter's algorithms will notice and you'll get the "Unable to Follow" notice fairly quickly.

And you don't have to follow your progress every few minutes. Inbetween following you've done all you can do for a few hours. So, hold off and forget about Twitter for a few hours. You'll get the same number of followers whether you obsessively check to see how many people are following you, or whether you just check a few times a day. Despite what I've just written you and I know when you first start you're going to check it about once a minute.

In the morning (6:00 A.M. – 8 A.M.) the first thing you'll do is followback everyone who has followed you overnight.

Then you want to start your new following using whatever criteria you've come up with. If you're following a topic, then pull up the topic and follow the most recent people for each topic. You might also check lists you're interested in and follow people from those lists. If you're following someone's followers start with their new followers, and then open the

URL for where you left off following further in their pages. Eventually you'll have a list of twitterers whose followers you follow regularly. If someone stops getting new followers you'll want to add to this list. Probably from the followers of new people you've followed after checking their followers to see if you have a lot of followers in common.

After you've followed 200 people go do something else for a few hours.

Around noon (12:00 P.M.) follow another 200 people using your standard procedure.

Don't forget to tweet during the day.

In early evening (6:00 P.M. P.M. – 7:00 P.M.) follow another 200 people.

Don't forget to tweet during the evening.

And by about 10:00 P.M. you'll probably be able to follow only a few more. Don't follow more than a hundred more. You don't want to get the "Unable to Follow" message at this point. If you do, you'll be limited until probably around noon the next day. Stopping following sooner rather than later gives your account a chance to rest for about 10 hours and all of Twitter's limits to reset.

If you follow this method you'll spend less than 30 minutes a day following people.

And, gasp, some days don't even bother to follow anyone. Go out and have fun. See a movie. Go for a hike. Don't become obsessive about how many followers you have on Twitter. Put life in perspective. Get out and about. And, of course, that might give you something to tweet.

Don't forget to tweet interesting things throughout the day. People might followback as a courtesy, but if they check your twitterstream and think it's lame they'll unfollow you. Be interesting, be helpful, be concerned, be friendly.

Checking Your Statistics

TwitterCounter (http://twitter.counter.com)

It's good to keep track of how many people followedback.

Go to TwitterCounter and put your [twitter_id] in and drag the URL into your bookmarks menu so you can pull up your TwitterCounter page just by clicking on the icon in your bookmarks menu.

This will bring up your statistics for the week (which is the default). You can click on buttons to see your Twitter statistics for the month, last three months, or last six months. The weekly/month/three months statistics are free. To see your six month statistics you have to subscribe to their service.

You can also check on other twitterers statistics, and even compare your statistics with someone else. TwitterCounter is a great service and I recommend it highly.

CHAPTER 6

TWITTER MANAGEMENT AND SCHEDULING

TWEEPI (TWITTER MANAGEMENT)

Managing Your Twitter Account

I use two websites to manage my Twitter accounts. I use Tweepi for managing my following and unfollowing, and Dynamic Tweets for scheduling my tweets in advance.

Tweepi (tweepi.com)

The Twitter management website I use is Tweepi. Without question the best Twitter management website I've found. I use it every day. They have both free and premium versions. I highly recommend them and have never been disappointed with them. They will make it easy to find followers and unfollow others. I considered this website a necessity for anyone wanting to manage their Twitter site without spending hours doing it. Can't write enough how great this site is.

There is a free version and various paid tiers. You can do everything in this book with the free version, but will probably want to upgrade to take advantage of some of their really cool search features in the premium versions.

Tweepi is important because you do not want to do any mass unfollowing from your Twitter account. You might not realize that you are doing it aggressively and might inadvertently violate Twitter's TOS. If that happens your account will be suspended. Tweepi has built-in safeguards to prevent you from exceeding Twitter's follow/unfollow limits.

Here are the Basic and Premium services Tweepi offers:

FOLLOW NEW TWEEPS (BASIC – FREE)

Follow followers

Follow your followers followers.

Follow friends

Follow those whom a friend are following.

Follow list

Follow users by following lists.

Paste & Analyze

Paste a comma separated list of twitterers into the search box and Tweepi will give you information about them in a table. Free version: 100 twitterers. Premium version: unlimited twitterers.

PREMIUM TOOLS (PAID)

Search & Follow

Search for twitterers by hashtag or keyword and then follow them.

Unfollow Them

Unfollow twitterers who have not tweeted for more than 30 days.

Flush Them

Unfollow twitterers whom you've followed 30+ days ago who have not followed you back.

Cleanup eggs

Cleanup twitterers who have not changed the default egg profile to their own profile.

Cleanup bio-less

Cleanup twitterers who have not added a biography in their description.

Cleanup – Klout-based

Clean up twitterers with a Klout Score less than 20 points (out of 100).

Once you login to Tweepi with Twitter's OAuth validation (and you can login one at a time with as many Twitter accounts as you have) Tweepi builds a list of whom you're following/who's following you/mutual followers. And they do it fairly quickly. I have a lot of followers and most management sites crash when I try to use them, not Tweepi.

Once they've accessed your Twitter account and indexed your followers, you have the ability to do everything you need to do in order to manage your Twitter account(s).

Safelist

There are some people whom you don't care if they follow you back. You still want to follow them and don't want to automatically delete them. Tweepi gives you the ability to create a safelist of all those whom you follow who don't follow you back, yet you don't want to delete. Then, even if you select everyone on a page and hit unfollow you will not unfollow those on your safelist.

Flush Unfollowers

Tweepi describes it as flushing unfollowers. When you click on that menu item Tweepi builds a list of those who aren't following you. A lot of times people will follow you and then after a week or so unfollow you in the hopes you won't notice. But, using Tweepi you'll notice.

Tweepi analyzes your followers and gives you the following information:

> You are following _ _ _ _ tweeps who are not following you back.

You have the option to Flush them, but not automatically. You can decide whom to flush and whom to keep, and possibly safelist. Because of Twitter's api you can't just click on the top checkbox and automatically check all those on the page (you used to be able to do that) and unfollow them. However, you can click on the top twitterer and hold down the shift key and then click on the last one to select all of them. Then you can hit unfollow and Tweepi unfollows everyone.

I've found the best way to do things is to go to the last page of unfollowers that Tweepi has created and work my way backwards. This means that I'm unfollowing the people who've had the longest time to follow me back. The more recent people will be at the beginning pages and might not have had time to follow me, so I want to give them time to do so before I delete them. By going to the last page and working my way back I'm certain that I'm unfollowing people who have had plenty of time to follow me back.

I usually leave the first 100 pages alone. That's about 2000 people whom I follow who aren't following me. This seems like a nice number. If you're following 300-500 (or even more) a day, then the 2000 represent those you've following in the last few days. So, it seems reasonable to give them 2-4 days to followback. And I don't actually unfollow every day. I do it maybe once or twice a week. The first time getting my unfollow list down to about 200 pages (that's with 20 on a page, or 4000). Then later in the week I'll unfollow to get that down to about 100 pages. There's really no need to do it every day. And I don't want to seem like I'm churning followers, since that's in violation of Twitter's Terms of Service.

Reciprocate (Follow Those Who Follow You)

You have several follow options. You can follow one of your followers' followers, their friends, or list members. I've found this useful in I'm following someone and we seem to have a lot of followers in common. I can determine this by going to that twitterer's page on Twitter and look at their followers. If I see a lot of their followers are already following me, then it's likely if I follow their followers a high percentage of them will follow me back. Likewise if I go to their page an find that virtually none of their followers is following me then it's unlikely there will be a high percentage following me back if I follow them.

_ _ _ _ tweeps are following you, but you're not following them back.

You have the option to Reciprocate and followback everyone who's following you.

Tweepi creates a list of all those who are following you whom you haven't followed back. You don't have to start at the oldest follower as you should when you Unfollow. Just start at the beginning and select all on a page and follow. And go through all the pages. Tweepi will take care that you don't exceed hourly follow limits.

You may find that you've followed someone who has protected their tweets. That means you've actually sent them a request to follow them. Tweepi will let you know. Just select the boxes for those who have protected their tweets and unfollow them. This cancels the request that was sent to them when you followed them. It won't affect their status following you. No sense in sending them a request to follow. They've protected their tweets because they only want friends to see their tweets. However, they do follow others whom they find interesting and obviously have followed you.

There are several informational columns you can turn on or off depending on whether or not you want to use the information in that column. The information can help you decide whether or not to follow someone. The columns show: Name, bio, location, # followers, # friends, #

statuses, Verified?, Protected?, Last tweet, # tweets, # replies, # RTs, # links, # FF, Klout Score, Links Ratio, Follow Ratio, Last Checked.

Obviously, if someone hasn't checked their Twitter account in weeks, or tweeted in three months they may not actually be logging on to Twitter often enough to see that you've followed them and to follow you back.

Probably the most important statistic is the person's Follow Ratio. This is the percentage of people the twitterer follows compared to those following them. If I have the time I'll go through and deselect those who have a 97% Follow Ratio and below. Obviously those with a 100%+ Follow Ratio are going to follow you back. If they have 85% or below chances are they're not going to. There are so many people to follow on Twitter I don't usually bother with those below a 97% Follow Ratio.

Follow Your Followers' Followers, Friends, Lists

You have several follow options. You can follow one of your followers' followers, their friends, or list members. I've found this useful in I'm following someone and we seem to have a lot of followers in common. I can determine this by going to that twitterer's page on Twitter and look at their followers. If I see a lot of their followers are already following me, then it's likely if I follow their followers a high percentage of them will follow me back. Likewise if I go to their page an find that virtually none of their followers is following me then it's unlikely there will be a high percentage following me back if I follow them.

Cleanup Options

Sometimes you might feel that you're following too many twitterers who tweet too much. You can clean up your twitterers.

You are following xxxxxx users, why not unfollow some

You can keep your account(s) nice and tidy by cleaning up some of your followers. You can go through and cleanup people whom you might not want to follow. Those who seem to be spammers, people who haven't tweeted in months, etc.

You can usually recognize spammers because they haven't added a bio or changed Twitter's default profile or background. You can also cleanup twitterers based on a low Klout score (see page 182).

Tweepi will help you increase your followers and save you lots and lots of time. Use it, sign up for the Premium services. This is the best online Twitter Management service. Even more so because most of it's free.

Dynamic Tweets (dynamictweets.com)

The other Twitter management tool I use, and recommend highly is Dyanmic Tweets.

Dynamic Tweets is a Twitter scheduling program. They have both free and pro accounts. You can schedule tweets, have multiple accounts, schedule intervals of scheduled tweets, bulk uploads, etc. Extremely business oriented.

I think their most important feature is the one that lets you do a bulk upload of tweets. You can create a comma delimited file of tweets and schedule date and times to be tweeted. Then you can bulk upload that file and Dynamic Tweets will post your tweets at the times you have scheduled. This is a wonderful feature. Worth all their other features combined.

This is the site I use to schedule tweets and I highly recommend them.

Twitter Counter (twittercounter.com)

This site gives you a graph of your Twitter statistics for the last week, month, 3-months, 6 months. Stats include followers, following, tweets, a combination of those three, mentions, retweets, your retweets, whom you're mentioning. And you can generate a graph comparing two different twitterers. They'll give you your Twitter ranking, and give you predictions based on your statics of how many followers you'll have in 30 days. Other predictions are various milestones like how many days until you reach 50,000 followers, or 100,000, etc.

CHAPTER 7

HOW TO SUCCESSFULLY INCREASE YOUR FOLLOWERS

INCREASING YOUR FOLLOWERS

Here are specific instructions on how to find twitterers to follow and then how to follow and, if necessary, unfollow them.

As I wrote earlier, you don't need any fancy programs to do this. You can use Tweepi as discussed in the previous chapter to find people to follow using various criteria.

High Followback Percentages

Notice all of these twitterers are followback Twitter accounts. I do have lists and lists of even higher percentage followback Twitter accounts. But because they are twitterer's personal accounts I'm not going to publish them in this book. However, if you pay for a one-year membership to a private website I've created you'll get access to Discussion Groups, Forums, template downloads for keeping track of your Twitter account(s), etc. I'll discuss specific individuals who have extraordinarily high followback percentages. Some as high was 95%. Additionally this book will be continually updated and if there are enough changes I'll give you a link to download a newer edition for free as part of your membership. All changes and updates will be posted on the website so you have the latest, greatest Twitter techniques. And you can share your stories, too. I'll answer questions and give helpful hints on how to be successful on twitter. And a one-year membership is only $10 (see page xvii).

Followback Twitterers

- twitter.com/teamfollowback (if you use only one of these sites, this is the one)
- twitter.com/afollow4follow
- twitter.com/follo4followers
- twitter.com/follow4follow
- twitter.com/ifollowbackTFB
- twitter.com/instantfollow
- twitter.com/te4mfollowb4ck
- twitter.com/willfollowback
- twitter.com/followback
- twitter.com/follow4follow
- twitter.com/ifollowbackuk

To find individual people to follow do an advanced Twitter search for:

- follow4follow
- ifollowback
- Followback

However target following by topics or things you're interested in will give you the most satisfying results. The above links are to give you quantity of followers.

See page 129 for information about advanced searches.

CHAPTER 8

HELPFUL WEBSITES

CAVEAT EMPTOR

Caveat emptor (let the buyer beware). Although I've made every effort to make certain the links throughout this book take you to active websites, I can't guarantee that a website will be up and running. They all were at the publication of this book. People discontinue websites all the time. Nor do I in any way endorse the use of any of these websites. Some might get your twitteraccount suspended. Please always use your Twitter account following Twitter's TOS.

I've mentioned the yearly membership to a private website for The Book of Twitter. I do keep all the links up-to-date on that website. And as soon as a link changes because a website has gone defunct, or I've found a better one, I change the ebook so that only the most recent updated version of the book is available for sale. If you do buy a yearly $10 subscription you will be able to download updated versions of this book throughout the year. And you'll be given new information from me and be able to join in discussions on Forums. For further information see page xvii.

There are several business-oriented URLs I have not included because I am still testing them to see if they work well enough to include. They will be available in any updates and on the website.

The following pages list a lot of really useful websites but is by no means complete. If you know of others, please let me know (yvettegr&hotmail.com). I'm always looking for interesting websites.

ALERTS

Pu.ly

pu.ly

Pu.ly is an email-to-Twitter-to-email client. You can send tweets via email and you'll be sent email alerts every time you receive a direct message on Twitter or mentions of your [twitter_id] by others on Twitter.

TweetBeep

tweetbeep.com

TweetBeep gives you *free* Twitter alerts by email referencing every time you're mentioned on Twitter. Both paid and free (with advertising) options. It's similar to Google Alerts only for Twitter.

Twilert

twilert.com

Twilert is a web app that sends email alerts of tweets containing keywords you specify. You may configure as many twilerts as you want, and configure each twilert to be sent at a specific time each day.

AUDIO/SOUND

AudioBoo

audioBoo.fm

Audioboo is a free service. It works from your iPhone or Android phone using downloadable apps. Or directly from your computer if you log onto audioboo.fm. You can record a message, attach a photo and location to that message and then upload it to Audioboo. A link for your Audioboo can automatically be tweeted from your Twitter account, or uploaded to facebook (and other social networking sites). Additionally you can upload already recorded sound files to your Audioboo account. Like Twitter you can follow people on Audioboo. You can also listen to other people's boos. Share on tumblr, facebook player, Posterous, friendfeed, etc. You can also use Audioboo's embed code. Additionally, you can podcast your feed or create an RSS feed.

Tweekly

tweekly.fm

Use Tweekly to post your last.fm music data and statistics to your Twitter and facebook accounts. You can do this automatically or manually.

BACKGROUNDS, FOLLOWME BUTTONS, BADGES, PERSONALIZED BACKGROUNDS

AddTwitter

addTwitter.com

AddTwitter creates an animated Follow Me button you can use on your blog or website.

MyTweetSpace

mytweetspace.com

Free as well as paid backgrounds, buttons, etc. Don't see what you want, they'll make it for you, for a fee. Prices start under $5.

TwBg

twBg.tweetbook.in

The twBg.tweetbook app creates a mosaic image of your friends, followers, or friends/followers on Twitter. You can easily install this image as your Twitter profile background using the app or doing it manual from your profile. You could also use it as wallpaper on your computer. Or, you can use it as a cover on a book (i.e., this book). There's an interesting option so you can use the image as a t-shirt you can order through zazzle.com. How cool is that? To wear a t-shirt of your followers?

TweetBacks

tweetbacks.com

Customizable free Twitter backgrounds.

TweetXilla

tweetxilla.com (formerly Twitterbackgrounds.com)

Free Twitter backgrounds.

Twilk

twilk.com

After you've logged on using Twitter's OAuth validation to give twilk access to your follower information they will be able to create a background from the profile pictures of people you follow, people who follow you, both people you follow and people who follow you, or people you follow who followback. You can create full color or B&W backgrounds using small, medium, or large images. The background image can fade from full color to black, left to right. You can create just a left sidebar of images with the right side black. The background images can be a series of squares, or a jumble of images that are square or rotated to the right or left. You can preview the background before hitting the "Use Background" button. Twilk has free and paid versions of backgrounds. The free version has an ad for Twilk in the upper left of your image, which makes it kind of prominent on your Twitter page. You have to subscribe ($5 per month/$40 per year) to the paid version, Twilk Pro, to get rid of their ad. In the paid version Twilk updates your background image throughout the month. There is a 30-day refund in case you decide you'd rather not use their services.

Twitter Buttons

twitterbuttons.com

Easy to use web app. Just input your [twitter_id] hit enter, and a window pops up with a button code you can use on facebook, your blog, etc. Lots of examples to choose from.

Twitter Gallery

twittergallery.com

Free Twitter backgrounds, buttons, avatars.

Twitter My Site

twittermysite.com

This site generates various Twitter button designs you can use on your blogs or websites to link to your Twitter account with style.

BLOGGING FROM TWITTER

BiggerTwitter

biggerTwitter.com

Just login to BiggerTwitter using Twitter's OAuth validation. There's a tweet box to type in your tweet. If you type in less than 140-characters you can just send it and it appears as a normal tweet. When you get beyond 140 characters and hit send Twitter will show up to 140 characters with a link back to BiggerTwitter for the rest of your messages. BiggerTwitter archives your messages so if someone finds your tweet in a few weeks it will still show up on BiggerTwitter.

Twitzer (ShortText)

shorttext.com

Twitzer is interesting in that it gives you two options for blogging with Twitter. The first is their Shortext site. No login is necessary. Designate whether your post will be public (default) or private. Create your blogpost using rich text if you want. There is a Firefox extension (http://shorttext.com/extension.aspx). You also have the ability to link images or video. You can designate your shorttext as private, in which case you put in a keycode (numerals, alphanumeric). You can also check a box to allow comments to your post. After you create your post type in the authentication code (different from the private code you create) and hit the "Create URL" button. It takes a little bit of time but eventually your shorttext URL will popup (with the private keycode you created if you wanted your post to be private). Copy the URL, login to Twitter and paste the URL as part of your tweet. The URL will remain active as long as you (or someone) visits your account on shorttext.com at least once a year. There will be advertising on the page unless you pay for an adfree URL. You may create as many shorttext posts as you want.

If you want to use ShortText as a Twitter client then you have to login to Twitter via OAuth validation. There's a Twitzer – Twitter long text login link at the bottom right of the screen.

Twitzer (Twitzer)

twitzer.com

This is the same as shorttext.com and installs as a FireFox extension and you use it from Twitter. Right now this extension is not available because it has not been updated to work with the latest version of FireFox. I will change this paragraph as soon as the extension has been updated.

Twitlonger

twitlonger.com

Their motto, "For when you talk too much for Twitter." Sign in with OAuth and then tweet from twitlonger. Write as much as you want. When you send the tweet they will add a link back to your tweet on twitlonger once you've reached the 140-character limit (including the link). You don't have to worry about counting characters, Twitlonger does it for you.

TwitWall

twitwall.com

Use Twitwall when 140 characters just isn't enough. TwitWall is a Twitter blogging companion that creates a link from Twitter to your TwitWall. You can embed videos, mp3 files or podcasts on your TwitWall. You can use bold, italic, center/left/right text. Of course what the other person sees on your tweet is some text and a link from Twitter to your TwitWall. You can't get around the actual 140-character feed and lack of graphics or audio/video files on Twitter.

BUYING TWITTER FOLLOWERS

I don't recommend that you buy Twitter followers. Generally it's expensive and you're just getting bodies, not targeted followers. And every once in a while Twitter clamps down on spammers and companies who use lists of followers they've made. Those followers will suddenly disappear from your Twitter account. So, ultimately, you wasted your money. I've only included a few here. Certainly there are a lot more.

More Twitter Followers

moreTwitterfollowers.com

Cheap site to buy Twitter followers. Seems to be mirrored at buyTwitterfollowers.info.

ViralSO

viralso.com/buy-Twitter-followers.html

Another place to buy Twitter followers.

COMMUNICATION

GroupTweet

grouptweet.com

GroupTweet is a free and paid service. GroupTweet gives you the ability to send private tweets to a group as DMs (Direct Messages). Those receiving the DMs can tweet back to the entire group. This is a great way to communicate if you're organizing something and want to tweet to everyone helping with the organization. You could send people updates on a rally without everyone in the twitterverse knowing about it.

It's great for target marketing, but only with opt-in lists.

It's great for family members to keep track of what everyone is doing.

Or, what if you've organized a wedding or party and want to notify people of any changes, especially on the day of the event. If you've created a group for everyone attending then you can notify everyone with one tweet.

DM @GroupTweet Bride wised up, came to her senses, ran away. You can get here late. We're still going to eat the cake. – Relieved Mom

You can create as many groups as you want. It works by sending one tweet to GroupTweet which then sends the tweet to everyone in your group.

CONTENT

Sometimes you just don't know what to tweet. Here are some places to get interesting information to tweet.

Brainy Quote

brainyquote.com

A great source of quotes to tweet. You can search by author, topic, event, etc. Find just what you need for what's happening that day.

Stuff to Tweet

stufftotweet.com

Remember, the best way to get followers is to be post interesting things so people will follow you and put you in their lists. However, sometimes you might just draw a blank on what to tweet. That's when you should try Stuff to Tweet. They list lots of current links that are popular elsewhere on the internet. These are already proven to be popular topics across the web that you might like to tweet about. See what's trending on Digg, Del.icio.us, Twitter, YouTube, Lifehacker, TMZ, Mashable, popular photos, WikiHow, Popular on CNN, Popular in the New York Times, Popular on Daily Motion, Popular Recipes, Popular on Amazon, Popular on Craig's List.

Trends24

trends24.appb.in

Trends24 is another website from tweetbook.in. This website lists trending topics from 5 minutes ago, 1, 2, 3, 4, 5, 6, 7, 8, 9, 10, 11, 12, 13, 14, 15, 16, 17, 18, 19, 20, 21, 22, and 23 hours ago. It's useful in case you have trouble knowing what to yweet. You can find popular topics at Trends24. Also you can see which trends have increased or decreased in popularity over the past 24 hours. A great way to tweet popular Twitter topics. You can also configure it to list Worldwide trends, trends by the United States or other countries, as well as specific American cities. Extremely useful tool.

Tweeting Too Hard

tweetingtoohard.com

Tweeting Too Hard's motto: Where self-important tweets get the recognition they deserve.

This site tracks pomposity on Twitter. Have you ever read a tweet and thought it was one of the most pompous things you've ever read? Well now you can submit that tweet to Tweeting too Hard and they'll post it in all it's solipsistic glory.

This site is hilarious. Here are some examples from Twitter.com/lisabarone, who seems particularly popular:

> Being smarter than everyone sure does get *exhausting* sometimes.
>
> I'm on Tweeting Too Hard AND Twouchebags this morning. God, I'm awesome.
>
> I wish I could tweet my food order in at Flavour. Taking my head phones off and walking to the counter is SUCH a burden.
>
> Keeping my nose in work today and ignoring most of you. It's not that I don't like you....wait, it's a little bit of that...
>
> Just tried on the dress I plan to wear to a wedding next month to ensure it looked like I remembered. Holy hell am I pretty sometimes.

And there's a handy button to retweet these tweets. Could make an interesting tweet for you every once in a while.

TwitSnip

twitsnip.com

TwitSnip was created by Hubspot.com. They also created Twittergrader (see page 185).

TwitSnip makes it very easy to "quote" text on any webpage and post it to your Twitter account. Just highlight/select some text you want to quote, click on the TwitSnip bookmarklet, check your post and then tweet it. Twitsnip looks up the @user for the website and links back to the source, shortening any URL's that need shortening. Of course your tweet still must stay within the 140-character tweet limit.

CONTENT DELIVERY

Dlvr.it

dlvr.it

Use Dlvr.it to automatically deliver content to Twitter, facebook, linkedin, googlebuzz, more. Gives you statistics about which of your social networks is getting the most attention. Uses bit.ly as their link shortener.

FOLLOW UNFOLLOW PROGRAMS

Tweet Adder

tweetadder.com and Tweeadder.com

Auto follow/unfollow program. Be very careful using third party software to add and delete followers. If you do it rapidly enough it's called churning. And churning is against Twitter's TOS. Twitter has said this sort of software can lead to account suspension.

The makers of software like this have put in safeguards to make certain they don't exceed Twitter's api limits. Software like this is very good at automating following targeted users, in addition to unfollowing those who don't follow you.

The software will work with multiple accounts in case you have more than one account. Also provides statistical analysis of your Twitter account.

It requires a one-time fee, with no monthly charges and comes with a lifetime license with unlimited upgrades. Available on Windows, Linux, and MAC platforms.

You can also upload tweets and also designate tweets to be sent to facebook and LinkedIn, in addition to Twitter.

Twidium

twidiumapp.com

Follow/Unfollow program only available on the Windows platform. You have to buy a yearly/2-yearly license. It allows for mass following (anybody), smart following (based on keywords), or list following (by topic). You can designate a schedule when to unfollow those who have not followed you back.

Twitter FriendAdder

livelybrowser.com/Twitter-Friend-Adder.html

Auto follow/unfollow program. Be very careful using third party software to add and delete followers. If you do it rapidly enough it's called churning. And churning is against Twitter's TOS. Twitter has said this sort of software can lead to account suspension.

The makers of software like this have put in safeguards to make certain they don't exceed Twitter's api limits. Software like this is very good at automating following targeted users, in addition to unfollowing those who don't follow you.

The software will work with multiple accounts in case you have more than one Twitter account and provides statistical analysis of your Twitter account(s).

There is a one-time fee, with no monthly charges. It comes with a lifetime license with unlimited upgrades.

URL-Link Shorteners (in alphabetical order)

Because of Twitter's 140-character limit they suggest you use link shorteners to compact links. And if you don't shorten your links

Twitter will do it for you automatically. Why not let them? Because some link shorteners provide you with analytics so you can see how many people have clicked on your link. Twitter doesn't do that.

I've used quite a few of the shorteners below but have pretty much settled on goo.gl because I like google, and I like the analytics and tracking available for my tweets. Also, I know goo.gl is not going anywhere so my URL's will be active next year. I've used some link shorteners that have disappeared in a year, or who've deleted my links after a while.

This paragraph is also earlier in this book. But, I think it's important to know how to put your shortened link in your tweet. Now for a really useful hint about putting a shortened link in your tweet. Put the shortened link at the start of your tweet. Then the rest of your tweet should deal with what the link is about. The reason for this is if you've put the link at the end of your tweet (like just about everyone does) and your tweet is retweeted and the retweet makes your tweet go over the 140-character limit your link will be truncated making it useless. If your link is at the start of your tweet and the retweet goes beyond 140 characters then the end of your tweet is cut off but the important link is okay.

Now what do those strange extensions mean. People are used to something being a .com, .net, .org, .edu. What's a .gl as in goo.gl? Obviously google wanted to use a gl to get as close to google as they could. But where did the .gl come from? It's the country code for Greenland. You'll also see a lot of people using .ly. Ly is the country code for Libya. Even if you live in the United States you don't have to use a United States country code (.us or the .com, .org. .net, .edu, et al). I've put the country code next to the extensions on the following link shorteners so you can see where they're coming from.

- adjix.com (United States)

- bit.ly (Libya)
- chilp.it (Italy)
- cli.gs (S. Georgia and S. Sandwich Islands)
- dld.bz (Belize)
- dot.tk (Tokelau)
- goo.gl (Greenland)
- is.gd (Grenada)
- j.mp (Northern Mariana Islands) (redirects to bit.ly)
- krz.ch (Switzerland)
- snipurl.com
- t.co (Colombia) This is twitter's link shortener. Each link is no more than 19 characters. However, it provides no analytics.
- tiny.cc (Cocos [Keeling] Islands)
- tinyurl.com (United States)
- tr.im (Isle of Man) (I like their motto: tr.im is a damn good name for a URL shortener)
- tweetburner.com (United States)
- twitthis.com (United States)
- twurl.nl (Netherlands) (leads to Tweetburner)
- urlborg.com (United States)
- urlShort.me (United States, becoming more popular for mobile apps. I like their pair of scissors favicon (the little icon next to a URL address in the browser's URL field).

LISTS

Listorious

listorious.com

This is a website about Twitter lists. Search for lists, add your own lists. A valuable resource for finding people and topics you're interested in. A fuller explanation of how to use listorious is earlier in this book (see page 130).

MONTIZING YOUR TWITTER ACCOUNT

ad.ly

ad.ly

An advertising site that will tweet ads that you've first approved. You designate categories that are appropriate to your twitterstream. When they have an advertiser that's interested in advertising on your channel ad.ly notifies you. You can read the ad and approve or disapprove. They tend to pay better than the other Twitter advertising sites by a country mile (see page 98).

Magpie

be-a-magpie.com

Submits advertising for your Twitter account for your approval. You can designate how many ads you want to run. You do not get paid until you've generated $50 in paid ads.

My Likes

mylikes.com

Get paid to share endorsements of products you like.

Revtwt

revtwt.com

Another site to monetize your Twitter account. Works pretty much the same as the other sites.

MANAGING FOLLOWERS

A lot of follow/unfollow sites pop up on the web. For the most part they appear very quickly and then disappear. They'll usually have the word "follow" in their URL: getfollowersfast.com, fastfollowers.com, etc. Both those URLs at one point promised you fast followers. They lasted a very short time.

You'll get better results following directly from Twitter. There are, however, some that are worthwhile, though being listed below is not meant to be an endorsement of any of the sites. The one service I use and do endorse is Tweepi. (see page 145 for an extensive explanation of how to use Tweepi.) If you have over 15,000 followers Tweepi is the only way to go. They don't crash at that many followers.

And be very careful when you follow/unfollow on Twitter. If you do it too aggressively Twitter considers that churning which is in violation of their Terms of Service and your account will most likely be suspended.

Fllwrs

fllwrs.com

Gives you information about who follows/unfollows you every day and will send you an email when someone unfollows you. Right now their service does not work for those with lots of followers.

Followerhub

followerhub.com

Follow-unfollow service for increasing your Twitter followers by following targeted twitterers and unfollowing those who unfollow you. Free and paid sections.

Friend or Follow

friendorfollow.com

Another Twitter manager. This site creates profile icons of those who follow you whom you don't follow, and those whom you do follow who don't follow you. You can click on a profile icon to follow the person or unfollow them. There is the option to export your lists as a .csv file. Doesn't work very well for accounts over 20,000.

ManageFlitter

manageflitter.com

Another Twitter cleaner. Follow those who follow you, unfollow those who don't follow you. You can also unfollow these accounts which seem to be inactive. There's a pro account available that allows you to do filtering and create a safelist.

Refollow

refollow.com

This site lets you unfollow, follow, block, lock, and unlock followers. It doesn't work with Twitter accounts with lots of followers. Probably not effective over 5000 followers.

Tweepi

tweepi.com

Without question the best Twitter management program. I use it every day. There are free and paid tiers. (see page 145 for an extensive explanation of how to use Tweepi.)

Tweet Big

tweetbig.com

Their Piggy Back feature analyzes followers of other users and identifies people for you to follow. You can also find potential followers based on keywords; automatically followback those who follow you; schedule how long you give someone to follow you back before you unfollow them; schedule future tweets; and analyze your followers. Both free and paid accounts. Not much functionality in the free version.

Twiends

twiends.com

An extremely interesting and effective way to get followers without buying them, though you can hurry things up by buying seeds (see page 115 for further information about Twiends). If you don't want to buy seeds there are plenty of ways to earn them. If you go to the Twitter tab you can follow people from there. Each follow is worth 0-9 sees. Nine is the most I've seen anyone offer. If you use up your Twitter follow limit for the day you can go to the YouTube tab and earn seeds by watching videos.

You put your value on the seeds you've earned/bought designating how much you're willing to spend on a follow. Two works well. Those seeds are immediately available for purchase by someone who agrees to follow you

Using this site is a very effective way to get followers. Then after you've got them manage them in Tweepi.

Twit Cleaner

thetwitcleaner.com

This site looks at your followers and gives you suggestions about them. Tells you the ones it thinks are spammers, those who seem to be bots of some sort, those who haven't tweeted in a while, and those whose tweets don't seem to have anything to do with your tweets. Then if you choose to do so you can clean up your twitterstream by easily unfollowing those Twit Cleaner suggests.

Twitter Karma

http://dossy.org/Twitter/karma

Twitter Karma will show follow/unfollow status of your Twitter account (see page 111 for further information). Doesn't work very well if you have over 15,000 followers. You might have to Whack! (reload) several times until it brings in all the data. But once you're at that many followers there are other better follow/unfollow sites. Make certain you check the box next to "Hide avatars?" right under the Whack! button. If you don't it'll take the program a loooooong time to assemble all your data because it's bringing in all those images too. This can be an extremely useful website for those just starting out on Twitter.

Twittollower

twittollower.com

Paid site for targeting followers. Works on autopilot.

Twollow

twollow.com

Find targeted Twitter followers using keyword searches. Can be used on multiple accounts. Gives you trends and analytics. Paid service.

Qwitter

useqwitter.com

Quitter sends you a daily list of everyone who unfollowed you that day. This site is produced and associated with Twittercounter.com.

Nearby Tweets

nearbytweets.com

As the name implies, people who are tweeting near you. You can also search for tweets at other locations and save those locations for future searches.

Tweetree

tweetree.com

You log onto Tweetree using Twitter's OAuth validation. This website puts your twitterstream in a tree format showing tweets from people who are replying to your tweets. Also shows external photos or video links in your twitterstream, not as links but as the actual pictures or videos. You can also tweet from the website.

POLLS & SURVEYS

twtpoll

twtpoll.com

Create polls and surveys and tweet a link to your polls. Free (400 responses), additional prices for other options including unlimited responses and public and private results.

TWEET BACKUPS

TweetBackup

tweetbackup.com

This website makes daily backups of your tweets. It's free, you just have to follow them (Twitter.com/@tweetbackup). You can export your backup as a csv file, text file, HTML, or RSS Feed.

Twimemachine

twimemachine.com

Generates a list of your last 3200 tweets.

Twitter (previous tweets)

http://twitter.com/[twitter_id]?page=2

Input the above URL and replace [twitter_id] with your Twitter user name (i.e. http://twitter.com/yvettegr?page=2).

Inputting page=2 takes you back two pages in Twitter history. Page=100 takes you back 100 pages. You can probably go back about 150 pages. You could always go back page=200, in which case you'll probably get no tweets. So try page=175, then 160, etc., until tweets start coming up. These will be the oldest tweets Twitter has available for you. However, Twitter never deletes any of your tweets. They do have everything you've ever tweeted in a massive database which at some point you'll have access too. Be careful what you tweet. Nothing ever disappears, including tweets you've deleted. And Twitter is continuously donating an archive of every tweet to the Library of Congress for future historians.

TweetBook

tweetbook.in

TweetBook is one of the best Twitter websites available. It creates a PDF eBook of your tweets. Does it quickly, and the resulting eBook looks very nice. The people behind TweetBook are also the creators of Trends24 (see page 164).

Tweetscan

tweetscan.com

When Tweetscan first loads it seems like a search engine. But if you look at the bottom line you'll see "Twitter Backup". Click on that and you'll find several backup options including: Your Tweets, Friends, Direct Messages, @Replies, Followers, Favorite Tweets. The Full Archive option backs up everything. This is one of the most complete backup archives available.

When Did You Join Twitter?

whendidyoujointwitter.com

Simple program that answers just one question: When did you join twitter. Type in your [twitter_id] and up will pop the date you joined.

TWEET SCHEDULERS

Brandchirp

brandchirp.com

Schedules tweets and finds Followers based on location or interest. Paid service

Dynamic Tweets

dynamictweets.com

Dynamic Tweets has both free and pro accounts (see page 151 for more information about Dynamic Tweets). You can schedule tweets, have multiple accounts, schedule intervals of scheduled tweets, bulk uploads, etc. Businesses will find this website very useful. Even non-business twitterers will find it useful. I use this service to schedule my tweets and recommend them highly.

HootSuite

hootsuite.com

HootSuite is one of our favorite Twitter schedulers. Free (has advertising) and pro plans. More than just a tweet scheduler, HootSuite gives you the ability to create groups, create a team and manage them, search for mentions of you or a topic, build analytics, and more. Feed your RSS feeds from HootSuite to all your social networks. HootSuite allows for multiple profiles in case you have more than one Twitter account. Works on desktop and mobile devices. A must.

Scheduling with HootSuite is quite easy. You can send tweets now, or schedule future tweets. And the niftiest scheduling feature lets you upload a .csv file of future tweets configured to send them via date and time. You don't have to input individual tweets in

HootSuite. This is the best feature of their website and can save you enormous amounts of time if you tweet a lot.

HootSuite supports Twitter, facebook, facebook pages, Linkedin, foursquare, MySpace, Wordpress.com, and Ping.fm.

SocialOomph

socialoomph.com (previously known as tweetlater.com)

This is a very nice Twitter management tool. There are free and paid versions. You can schedule tweets and track keywords. There are extended Twitter profiles so you can promote yourself, Uses the dld.bz link shortener. You can also set your account to auto-follow and auto-DM those who follow you. Lots of other Twitter capabilities.

Timely

timely.is (previously known as whoshouldifollow.com)

Timely is a free Twitter scheduler with a difference. Instead of scheduling a specific time for your tweets you let Timely do that, and they'll publish them when they're most likely to have the highest impact. That means you'll get more retweets, mentions, and hopefully followers. The more you tweet the more their analysis of your tweets improves.

TWITTER ANALYTICS AND STATISTICS

NEOFORMIX.COM

Neoformix has several analytics programs aimed at twitterstreams.

Twit Arcs

neoformix.com/Projects/TwitArcs/TwitArcs.html

Enter a [twitter_id] (using the @ before the id, i.e., @yvettegr), or a search term. TwitArcs creates an arc based on the [twitter_id] or search term. The arcs on the left connect people that are repeated. The arcs on the right are for common repeated terms.

Twitter Spectrum

neoformix.com/Projects/TwitterSpectrum/TwitterSpectrum.html

Enter two comparison terms. If they are just words then separate them by a comma:

up,down

If they are [twitter_id]s then use this format:

from:yvettegr,from:gnomesatwork.

Twitter Spectrum compares the two terms.

Twitterstream Graphs

neoformix.com/Projects/TwitterStreamGraphs/view.php

Shows a streamgraph of the latest 1000 tweets which contain whatever search word you input. Underneath the streamgraph are the most recent tweets with your keyword in them. The resulting graph will show words associated with your search term. You can click on a word in the streamgraph to create a new streamgraph using that word.

Twitter Topic Explorer

tweettopicexplorer.neoformix.com

It will retrieve recent tweets from the [twitter_id] you input. The site creates a graphic of circles of various sizes and colors representing the words in recent tweets. Very interesting visuals about a person's tweets.

Twitter Venn Diagram

neoformix.com/Projects/TwitterVenn/view.php

Creates a Venn diagram based on two or three search terms (separated by comma's) that you enter. The resultant Venn diagram shows the rate of tweets containing your search terms.

Awe.sm

awe.sm (The sm stands for San Marino)

Analytics for social media aimed at businesses. It's a paid service, but there is a 30-day free trial to try it out and see if it's useful for you or your company. Analyzes your facebook and Twitter impact.

Backtweets

backtweets.com

An analytics site that analyzes your tweets and how people are interacting with you on Twitter.

Followerwonk

Followerwonk.com

Twitter Analytics. Search Twitter Bios gives you options to search biographical information by location or name(s). Compare Uses compares up to three twitterers. Comparisons include whom they follow or their followers. Slice 'n Dice compares whom a twitterer follows or who follows them. You buy services based on credits. You earn credits by being logged on, following them on facebook, or tweeting about them. You also earn credits every hour of the game. And you can buy credits

Klout

klout.com

Ever wonder how much clout you have on Twitter? Now you can find out at klout.com. Just type in your [twitter_id] and Klout will give you all kinds of information about your twitterstream as well as a Klout rating/score.

Rowfeeder

rowfeeder.com

Another statistical analysis site to track keywords, #hashtags, or users. Works with Twitter & facebook. Reports can be downloaded and opened in either Excel or Numbers. There are free and paid versions.

Socialbro

socialbro.com

Currently they are in beta. But the services they will be offering include browsing your followers, easy followback, track who has unfollowed you, backup your Twitter followers and friends (this seems like a sensational feature), statistical information, filter and sort your followers/friends; easy unfollow; manage Twitter lists; Tweet or DM friends/followers based on search results; see your twitterverse in a map.

TFF Ratio

tffratio.com

Shows your TFF (Twitter Follower-Friend Ratio) and some other statistics about your Twitter account.

Tweepletwak

tweepletwak.com

Keep track of who unfollows you. Keep statistics on who's following and unfollowing you. If you like they'll send a message to those who unfollowed asking why.

TweetReach

tweetreach.com

TweetReach gives you metrics for your tweets. Post a tweet and TweetReach will give you statistics on how many people viewed it and who they were, even listing the number of unique users who saw your Tweet. Great for marketing campaigns, contests, and to keep track of how successful your tweets are.

Tweetpsych

tweetpsych.com

This website looks at your tweets and comes up with a psychological profile of you, and then lists other twitterers who think like you. (That's such a scary thought!) Don't take it seriously. It was way off base with it's analysis of me. Or at least that's what the voices tell me.

Tweetspinner

tweetspinner.com

Tweetspinner has Basic, Advanced, and Pro accounts. It automatically de-spams/archives your DM inbox to their system. Schedules rotation of Twitter profiles & designs. They also have sophisticated follower management tools and analytics.

Tweetstats

tweetstats.com

Type in your [twitter_id] and up will pop charts that have graphed statistics about your Twitter name. All sorts of things you'd never even think to think about. Very interesting.

Tweetvalue

tweetvalue.com

Just type in your [twitter_id] and tweetvalue will figure up it's value.

Trendistic (twist.flaptor.com redirects to Trendistic)

trendistic.com

Tracks trends on Twitter. You can even input your [twitter_id] and it'll show you a graph of your tweets over several days. Or put in a topic, or news item and see how those things have trended.

Trendrr

trendrr.com

Paid service (14-day free trial) that tracks trends and statistics about your company/brand.

Twitalyzer

twitalyzer.com

Statistics and analytics about your twitterstream

Twitter Counter

twittercounter.com

This is repeated earlier in this book in Chapter6. This site gives you a graph of your Twitter statistics for the last week, month, 3-months, 6 months. Stats include followers, following, tweets, a combination of those three, mentions, retweets, your retweets, whom you're mentioning. And you can generate a graph comparing two different twitterers. They'll give you your Twitter ranking, and give you predictions based on your statics of how many followers you'll have in 30 days. Other predictions are various milestones like how many days until you reach 50,000 followers, or 100,000, etc.

Twitter Friends

twitter-friends.com

Still a Twitter-friends.com URL, but they've changed their name to Tweetmetrics. Gives you statistics about Twitter and your twitterstream.

Twitter Grader

twittergrader.com

TwitterGrader was created by Hubspot.com (an online marketing company with lots of excellent advice – highly recommended). They also created TwitSnip (see page 165).

TwitterGrader.com (also Twitter.grader.com) measures your influence on Twitter. Just type in your [twitter_id] and after a few moments your grade pops up. My grade was 100 out of 100, Rank of 148 out of 9,558,702. Next are your followers/following/updates numbers. After that there's an account summary of your Twitter account. It lists the day you signed onto Twitter (for me April 17, 2008, 17:17:16 (16 seconds after 5:17 in the afternoon). And you can click on a link to see others who signed up when you did. You can click on Follower History to see a graph of trends for your Twitter site. You can also enter someone else's [twitter_id] and check to see if they are following you.

Twitaholic

twitaholic.com (Twitterholic redirects to twitaholic.com)

Shows the top 100 twitaholics based on followers in each state. Also has a national list of the top 1000 Twitaholics.

The Twitter Tag Project

theTwittertagproject.com/milestone.php

Mr. Milestone does something very simple. He sends you a tweet when you hit a milestone 100 followers, then every 100 followers until you hit a thousand; 1000 followers, then every time you add another 1000 followers. All you have to do is follow Twitter.com/mrmilestone. If you want to stop receiving the milestone tweets all you have to do is unfollow mrmilestone.

Assetize

assetize.com (redirects to visibli.com)

Tracks the links you share on Twitter and how many views they've received. You can get a list of all the links you've posted in the last week, how many clicks total for all your links, and your links listed by order of popularity.

TWITTER CLIENTS

Destroy Twitter

destroyTwitter.com

Destroy Twitter is a Mac or PC Twitter client that runs through Adobe Air. It has menu buttons for: Home, Mentions, Search, and Messages. An "Away" button at the bottom right pauses the twitterstream. There's a thought balloon to the right of the "Away" button to bring up a 140-character tweet window. There's a popup menu of link shorteners to use with any links. Your choices are: j.mp, bit.ly, is.gd, tinyurl.com. You can also upload files from: Posterus.com, twitgoo.com, img.ly, Plixi, Imgur, Pikchur, Twitpic, Yfrog.

Echofon for Twitter (formerly Twitterfon)

echofon.com

Echofon is a Twitter client for the iPhone, iPad, and Mac. There's also a Firefox extension. And soon there will also be Windows support. You can view friends, followers, send tweets, reply to messages, upload photos to twitpic.com, etc. A nice feature is that it syncs your read tweets between your iPhone, desktop, and iPad. The app will notify you of any mentions or messages that have been sent to you. There are free downloads for your iPhone, iPad, and Mac (soon for Windows).

Hahlo

hahlo.com

Hahlo is a Twitter client optimized for the iPhone. Also works on your desktop, in Safari, Chrome, and Firefox.

Shareholic

shareholic.com

Tweet and share links from your browser. Supports Firefox, Google Chrome, IE8, Safari, Opera.

SocialToo

socialtoo.com

Socialtoo is a Twitter Management Client that lets you:

- Autofollow those who follow you
- Sync your Follows
- Block automatic DMs from other services
- Send out your own automatic DM to anyone who follows you

A few of the services are free, but there's a monthly fee for total access.

Tweetcaster

tweetcaster.com

Twitter client from handmark.com for iPhone, Android, and Windows phones. Displays tweets, profiles, and links. Other functions include (though not available on all platforms):

- "Zip It" Functionality
- Instapaper Support
- Color Code Tweets
- facebook Integration
- Multiple Widgets

- Multi-Account Support
- Twitter Lists
- Tweet Filtering
- Integrated Retweets
- Notifications Offline Tweet Caching
- Photo Attachment

TweetDeck

tweetdeck.com

TweetDeck has long been the premiere Twitter client. Even Twitter thought so since they just bought TweetDeck. It's a Twitter client that lets you peruse Twitter, facebook, more. Works on your desktop (MAC and PC), iPhone, iPad, Android, Chrome, etc. Has a directory of top twitterstreams by category.

URL shorteners include (in alphabetical order):

- bit.ly
- is.gd
- tinyurl.com
- Tr.im
- twurl.nl

Twit Scoop

twitscoop.com

Shows the twitterstream, direct messages to you, your replies, hot trends, search, and bookmarks.

Twitter for iPhone

twitter.com/#!/download/iphone

Twitter client from the Apple app store for the iPhone, iPod touch, and iPad. Requires IOS 3.1 or later.

Twitterrific

twitterrific.com

MacWorld 2010 Twitter Client of the Year. For the Mac, iPad, and iPhone.

Uber Social

bb.ubersocial.com/bb/download.php

Twitter client developed specifically for the Blackberry.

Blackbird

http://dossy.org/twitter/blackbird/

A very nice Blackberry Twitter client.

WordTwit Pro

bravenewcode.com/wordtwit

Brand new WordPress Twitter client from Brave New Code. Both free and paid accounts.

Tweetmeme

tweetmeme.com

Hottest links on Twitter.

Twemes

twemes.com

Twitter memes, global tags for Twitter.

Twitturls

twitturls.com

Lists the most tweeted links.

Twitturly

twitturly.com

Twitt(url)y tracks URLs that are currently being tweeted on Twitter. Much like Digg.com, people vote on a URL. More votes = higher ranking. However, you don't actually have to vote. Twitturly automatically tracks all the links people send on Twitter and ranks the most popular posted links. You can use twitturly to see trends and tweet those trends to raise your visibility and increase your popularity. Join in on popular conversations and you'll start to get noticed. Tweet something interesting about the URL and include it to get noticed.

TWITTER RESOURCES)

Twitter has a lot of resources you can use for free at http://twitter.com/about/resources.

Follow Button

http://twitter.com/about/resources/followbutton

You can use this customized follow button on your website/blog so that people can follow you from your website/blog.

Tweet Button

http://twitter.com/about/resources/tweetbutton **(to create a Tweet Button)**

http://dev.twitter.com/pages/tweet_button **(to further customize a Tweet Button)**

You can put this button on your website, click on it and post tweets from your website.

Twitter Logos and Icons

http://twitter.com/about/resources/logos

A page of Twitter logos and icons that you can use on your website or blog. Downloadable both as .png and vector images.

Twitter Widgets

http://twitter.com/about/resources/widgets

Puts your twitterstream on your website or facebook page

TWITTER SEARCH (TOPICS AND FOLLOWERS)

Cheap Tweet

cheaptweet.com

This search engine lets you search for deals or sell merchandise. You can look for deals to buy (paid); or advertise your deals in the sidebar (paid). You can post listings of items you have for sale for free. Just post your item details on Twitter using the #cheaptweet hashtag.

Social Searching

socialsearching.info

This search engine is really unique. Twitter's search engines (and most others) let you only search back two weeks. This one lets you search all tweets. You must sign in with a Twitter to use it. It also has a facebook search option.

Twazzup

twazzup.com

Twitter search client. Type in a topic and you'll receive a list of tweets that reference that topic.

Tweetcloud

tweetcloud.com

There are two search fields, one for a keyword search, and the other for a user search.

TweetFind

tweetfind.com

Paid service ($19/year to be listed), searching is free. Twitter Directory with Social Listings, Lists and Tools. Also gives live Twitter search results of people who aren't in their directory.

Tweet Grid

tweetgrid.com

Create multiple grids and search for different topics in each grid. The grids update live as new tweets are recorded on that topic. You can save search grid combinations and reload them whenever you want. Watch their video at http://vimeo.com/2356559.

Twellow

twellow.com

This is the Twitter yellow pages (yellow + Twitter = twellow). Use it to find people by topics. Makes it so you can find potential targeted followers. Great resource.

Twibes

twibes.com (twibe.com redirects to twibes.com)

To use twibes you set up an account and set up your profile with ten areas of interest. Twibes uses Twitter's OAuth validation so you don't have to give them your login or password information (if a service asks for that, then go elsewhere). You can search for twibes members by name, profession, topics, threads, lists, or groups. If you don't see a list or group for your interest, you can start one. Twibes monitors your tweets to keep track of the keywords you use and tries to match you with others who use the same keywords. You can tweet directly from twibes to your entire twitterstream or only twibes members.

Twibes is one of the best sites available for finding targeted followers. You can follow them on Twitter at Twitter.com/twibes

Twitbin (Firefox Extension)

twitbin.com

As Firefox writes: Twitbin is a Firefox extension that allows you to keep up with all of your Twitter conversations right from your browser sidebar. Send messages, receive messages, share links, and more from Twitbin, the best Twitter extension for Firefox out there.

Twitpipe

twitpipe.com

A simple website that lets you search for tweets containing up to three search terms within up to 100 miles (also 100 km) of a location. Great if you're traveling and want to find a restaurant recommendation in your area, or something interesting to do.

Twitter (two search engines)

search.twitter.com

Twitter's general search engine. Once you link to it you'll get a field to enter your search term(s). Searches only go back the previous two weeks. Searching for yourself is an easy way to see if anyone has asked you a question or responded to one of your tweets. Or, to see what other people are saying about you. Once you put your name in the search field and Twitter does a search, drag the URL from your browser to your bookmarks bar. That way you just have to click on that bookmark which already has you as a search term and you'll skip the step of having to input your name. You can also do this for any category you want to follow by dragging the URL to your bookmarks bar and just clicking on it when you want to repeat the search.

Here's the search parameter that Twitter uses:

```
http://search.Twitter.com/search?q=[searchterm]
```

For example to search for me you'd put in:

```
http://search.Twitter.com/search?q=yvettegr
```

To search for cupcakes you'd put in:

```
http://search.Twitter.com/search?q=cupcakes
```

If your search has more than one term, use an underline where the space is:

http://search.Twitter.com/search?q=cupcake_recipes

twitter.com/invitations/find_on_Twitter

Twitter search by Name, Interests, Organizations, Suggestions For You, Find Friends, Invite by Email. This only finds people/organizations that currently have Twitter accounts.

Twitterfall

twitterfall.com

Twitterfall lets you search for tweets (using filters if you choose) by current trends on Twitter and view them in a "waterfall" in the center of your browser. You can tweet from the interface and view your own Twitter timeline, including mentions and DMs.

TwitterFountain

twitterfountain.com

TwitterFountain is a visually fun way to view tweets. Select a category and a stream of tweets will start scrolling Star Wars style and the changing background will be images that share the same tags as the scrolling tweets. Very interesting.

Twittervision

twittervision.com

Twittervision shows a map with popups of tweets from the map you are viewing. You can let it use your location and you'll see things being tweeted nearby. Or you can select any part of the world to see tweets that are being tweeted from that part of the world. Very interesting.

Twtrfrnd

twtrfrnd.com

Twtrfrnd is a simple website that lets you compare your site with someone else's to see how many followers you both have in common. A high rate in common would indicate that this person's followers would have a high followback rate if you follow them since you have similar interests.

VALIDATION

TrueTwit

truetwit.com

Truetwit is a validation service that some twitterers use to validate that the person following them is a real person, isn't a spammer, etc.

Before you are accepted as a follower of someone registered with Truetwit, truetwit will DM you a validation link. When you click on it you'll be taken to Truetwit's page where you can sign up for their service or fill out the captcha form at the bottom so you are validated for the person you attempted to follow.

I don't use Truetwit (other than to answer a validation request) because I think it discourages followers. Right now if someone follows me they just show up as a followers. But if I were registered with Truetwit they would have to go through the validation process. A lot of people have no idea what Truetwit is so they won't respond, possibly thinking it's spam, in which case I've lost a follower. Other people just find it intrusive and irritating. So, either way you're going to lose potential followers.

I haven't had problems with spammers. Of course, they're there for a brief time, but Twitter has gotten very good about deleting spammer accounts, usually within a couple of days of them signing up for Twitter. Spammers used to be much more of a problem.

We Follow

wefollow.com

Wefollow works a lot like twibes. You add your interests or specialties and are listed in those categories. Then others can find your category and follow you. Or you can search in categories/topics and find others to follow. This is a way to target followers who have similar interests to yours which means a high followback percentage.

VIDEO

Twitcam

twitcam.com

You can't actually stream live video on twitter, but you can send links to a livestream from Twitcam in just three easy steps:

- Connect your webcam
- Login with Twitter
- Click the broadcast button

When you hit the broadcast button a video description and link for your video is posted to Twitter. You can even interact with your Twitter followers live while you're broadcasting. After your video feed is finished Twitcam archives it for you.

CHAPTER 9

GLOSSARY, ABBREVIATIONS, AND SMILEYS

When you first signup on Twitter and begin tweeting and receiving tweets you might find the language confusing because over the years a certain vernacular has evolved in the twitterverse. Here's a guide to the words of the twitterverse to help you.

I have also included some of the more popular abbreviations and smileys. However, I will have a book (also iPhone and Android apps) out soon that has a comprehensive list of abbreviations and smileys. Email me (yvettegr@hotmail.com) if you're interested in receiving a notification about it.

If you come across any words I've left out in the glossary, please let me know so I can include them in future editions of this book.

The Glossary and Abbreviations have been combined into one section, the Smileys are at the end of the Glossary. I would certainly recommend you use Abbreviations and Smileys sparingly. Too much of a good thing, you know. Also, a lot of people may not know what you mean by the Abbreviation or Smileys you use (in which case tell them about this book).

GLOSSARY

ABBREVIATIONS AND SMILEYS

.@[twitter_id] (notice the dot in front of the @ sign): This is how you configure a public reply to a specific person, but have that reply show up throughout Twitter. If you want the reply to only show up in the twitterstream of those who follow you and the person you are replying to, then drop the dot in front of the @ sign.

@[twitter_id]: This is how you configure a public reply to a specific person. This reply will be seen only by those who follow you and the person you are replying to. If you want the tweet to be tweeted to everyone then put a dot before the @ sign: .@[twitter_id].

#BeMyGuest: The bemyguest hashtag gives others permission to use your tweet and perhaps swap ideas about the topic.

#FF, #FollowFriday (Follow Friday, Friday Follow): Every Friday twitterers send out tweets suggesting others to follow for no other reason than they think they're interesting and deserve to be followed. The #FF hashtag is more popular than #FollowFriday just because it takes fewer characters.

#FollowLocals: Hashtag to suggest local twitterers should follow these other local Twitters. FollowLocals without the hashmark is also used (see page 206).

#hashtags: A hashtag is a tagged term to designate a trending topic on Twitter, event or location. You place the (#) symbol in front of your tag in order to designate it as a hashtag. They are usually placed at the end of a tweet and you can use more than one in a tweet. For example you might want to designate your tweet as about popcorn:

You can never have too much butter on your popcorn. #popcorn #butter

If someone searches for popcorn or butter your tweet will come up. If someone only wants to find a tweet about popcorn and butter then your tweet will come up. If someone only has a popcorn or a butter hashtag their tweet will not show up. The drawback to adding hashtags to your tweet is that they take away from your 140-character tweet count. You'll have to shorten your tweet to accommodate any hashtags.

#**NF:** Hashtag for New Follow.

A

AB/ABT: about (abbreviation)

adventuritter: an adventurous twitterer

Api (Application Programming Interface): An interface used to build applications. Platforms have api's specific to their programming. Twitter has it's own api, facebook has it's, Apple has an api, etc.

attwaction: an attraction you feel towards another twitterer

attwacker: someone who attacks someone on Twitter. Obviously since it's all digital they're attacking them with words. Because there isn't really human interaction people will type out things they'd never say while arguing with a person in real life. So dial it back a little on your own tweets, and hopefully that'll influence others. If you do criticize others for being a bit overbearing be prepared to be a victim of their wrath. They've already shown they can attack others, and they'll gladly attack you. Some people are trolls and enjoy attacking people over the internet because they think it's fun. They aren't really very nice people.

attwicted: addicted to Twitter

avatar: Your Twitter profile picture. It can be of you or anything you want to represent your twitterstream. Instructions on changing your profile picture are given on page 42.

B

B: be (abbreviation)

BBL: Be Back Later (abbreviation)

B/C: because (abbreviation)

B4: before (abbreviation)

backtwound: The background on your twitterstream.

beertweet: A tweet sent under the influence of beer, and one that you usually regret. Similar to drunk dialing in real life. And like drunk dialing you can't take it back. See also drunktwittering, drunktweeting, dweet.

BFN: Bye for Now (abbreviation). For when you are temporarily going away.

bird-of-mouth: Spreading information through tweets. The Twitter equivalent of word-of-mouth. Usually you hope bird-of-mouth tweets are spread from twitterer to twitterer and reach a huge audience.

block: You have the ability to block any twitterer from following you. Just go to their Twitter page and in the dropdown follow/unfollow menu there is also the option to Block them. If you change your mind later you can Unblock them.

BTW: by the way (abbreviation)

C

celebritweet: A tweet by a celebrity or their co-twitterer or ghost twitterer.

celebtwit: A celebrity on Twitter. They may or may not do their own tweeting. See also celebritweet.

CLD: could (abbreviation)

co-twitterer: Someone who has been given permission to tweet from someone else's Twitter account. A lot of celebrities and politicians use co-twitterers because they don't actually have time to tweet. Or, more probably, don't want to tweet but want to have a Twitter presence, so they use a co-twitterer. Ghost twitterer is explained later (see page 208).

commutweet: A tweet from a train, plane, bus while you're commuting. Flitter is a similar term (see page 206).

CRE8: create (abbreviation)

CT (cuttweet): A tweet that has to be shortened in order to be retweeted. If you have the space it's good twitiquette to put CT in the tweet to let others know it differs from the original. And if they know that and you've included the @[twitter_id] (also considered good twitiquette) of the original poster they can do a search to find the original tweet. MT (modified tweet) is another option to tell people the tweet has been changed (see page 206).

cuttweet (CT): A tweet that has to be shortened in order to be retweeted. If you have the space it's good twitiquette to put CT in the tweet to let tweeple know it differs from the original. And if they know that and you've included the @[Twitter ID] (also considered good twitiquette) of the original poster they can do a search to find the original tweet.

D

deets: details (abbreviation)

Deja-Tweet: A tweet that you swear you've read before.

detweet: A tweet you've cancelled before you've posted it because you thought better of it.

Direct Message (DM), pl. Direct Messages (DMs): If your tweet begins with DM @[twitter_id] (the person you're tweeting) then your message will be sent privately to the other person. It doesn't show up in your twitterstream. You can only DM someone you mutually follow. If you follow them, but they don't follow you, or they follow you but you don't follow them, then you can't DM them. This is the reason you should followback everyone who follows you. It's the only way you can engage in a private conversation with them.

DM (Direct Message), pl. DMs (Direct Messages): If your tweet begins with DM @[twitter_id] (the person you're tweeting), then your message will be sent privately to the other person. It doesn't show up in your twitterstream. You can only DM someone you mutually follow. If you follow them, but they don't follow you, or they follow you but you don't follow them, then you can't DM them. This is the reason you should followback everyone who follows you. It's the only way you can engage in a private conversation with them.

drive thru tweet: Tweeting while waiting in the drive thru at a fast food restaurant.

drive-by-tweet: A very quick tweet you squeeze in while doing other things

drunktwittering, drunktweeting: The Twitter version of drunk dialing usually to an ex you haven't gotten over that you contact while drunk. See also **beertweet, dweet.**

dweet: A drunken tweet sent while drunk. Equivalent to drunk dialing.

DYK: did you know (abbreviation)

E

eavestweeting: Eavesdropping on a Twitter conversation and then popping in uninvited with your own opinion.

egotwistical: A twitterer who tweets mainly about themself. Narcissitwit is another similar term (see page 212).

emergatweet/emergetweet: A desperate 911 tweet sent out from your twitterstream when you can't call 911. Give specific details of the emergency help you need. If you can turn on Twitter's geolocate feature and your location will be associated with the tweet. So if you're name is Timmy and you're trapped in a well and Lassie isn't around, Twitter can come to your rescue. It won't be helpful if you just tweet that you need help. Do not send out an emergatweet/emergetweet as a joke. It is taken seriously and concerned readers might go so far as to try to trace your location. You may find emergency personnel on your doorstep and they won't be happy if you were just joking.

exactotweet: A tweet that is exactly 140 characters. Not recommended because it makes it hard for someone to retweet. Always allow characters for your @[twitter_id] and RT. So if "RT @[twitter_id]" is 14 characters (including spaces before and after, then make certain your tweet is no more than 126 characters.

F

fa-btweeting: A term that means you're tweeting on facebook and Twitter at the same time. You can do this using software, Twitter clients, or websites.

fabetweet: A tweet that doesn't make a whole lot of sense, but tries to be funny.

Fail Whale: A drawing by Yiying Lu (see page 100) that shows a whale being lifted by bluebirds. It appears on your screen when Twitter is down. Just refresh your browser and it usually goes away. It's very temporary, sometimes lasting only seconds. It's because Twitter sometimes increases membership faster than they increase bandwidth so the Fail Whale appears. But, it is rapidly carried away by Twitter birds. Other fail screens are shown on pages following the Fail Whale.

Favorite: Twitter gives you an option of favoriting a tweet (comparable to bookmarking a URL) (see page 134).

flitter: A tweet made from an airplane. Commutweet is another term also (see page 203).

Follow: The act of clicking the follow button to follow someone's tweets. In order to receive a twitterer's tweets in your twitterstream you have to follow them. They don't have to followback. But, if you want to send DMs (Direct Messages) to each other then you both have to mutually follow each other. Following someone is similar to "friending" someone on facebook.

Followorthy: A tweet suggesting to others that @[twitter_id] is followorthy. The term derives from the Seinfeld episode in which Elaine has to figure out if someone is spongeworthy.

Followback: When someone follows you and you reciprocate it's known as followback. Some tweeple don't do it. I, however, followback everyone who follows me. The reason is that you can only engage in private conversation (DM's, Direct Messages) with someone if you mutually follow each other. Otherwise if you try to DM someone who doesn't follow you you'll get a message saying you can't do that. The alternative is to just reply to send them a message or reply to their tweet. But this will be public, so don't make it something that you don't want everyone in the twitterverse to read.

Follow Friday (#FF, Friday Follow): Every Friday twitterers send out tweets suggesting other tweeple to follow for no other reason than they think they're interesting and deserve to be followed.

FollowLocals: Hashtag to suggest local twitterers should follow these other local Twitters. #FollowLocals is another version (see page 200).

Followers: This is the section in the sidebar that lists everyone who is following you. These are the tweeple who have followed/subscribed to your twitterstream so that your tweets show up in their twitterstream. It is good form to reciprocate and followback anyone who has followed you.

Following: This is the section in the sidebar that lists everyone you're following. Ideally your Followers/Following should be fairly equal since you want to reciproate and follow anyone who follows you. Some tweeple might have made their tweets private, in which case you can't follow them even though they can follow you (because your tweets are public).

Followluv: This is when you give shootouts in a tweet naming some of your new followers encouraging others to follow them. If you do this on Friday use the #FF (Follow Friday) #hashtag. Other days just give the shoutout in a tweet. You might do this because someone has done you a favor, or you just like what they've been tweeting. It's done without any expectation of reward. Though, if you do it a lot you'll find that others are giving shoutouts to you. And shoutouts can result in increasing your followers.

Followpalooza: Everyone once in a while you might find yourself all of a sudden you're getting a lot of followers. Usually it's in response to something you've tweeted that has been retweeted a lot of times and tweeple have discovered your twitterstream and like you. Think of it as hitting the Twitter jackpot for that day. See Friendapalooza.

Foul Owl: If you go to a follower's twitterstream and find their account has been suspended you'll see the orange Foul Owl (see page 101). Accounts are suspended for Terms of Service violations. Things like harassing someone, churning their account (repeatedly following/unfollowing them), posting copyrighted material, etc. The Foul Owl along with the Blue Bird mascot, and the Fail Whale are animals used by Twitter to represent Twitter. The Foul Owl and Fail Whale both mean something is wrong with the page you're accessing (either Twitter is down or that page is down by suspension).

Freaking Tweeting (Freakin' Tweetin'): A barrage of tweets from a twitterer who has obviously lost control and is tweeting uncontrollably, and usually without making a whole lot of sense.

Friday Follow (#FF, Follow Friday): Every Friday twitterers send out tweets suggesting other tweeple to follow for no other reason than they think they're interesting and deserve to be followed.

Friendapalooza: Every once in a while you might find yourself all of a sudden getting a lot of followers. Usually it's in response to something you've tweeted that has been retweeted a lot of times and tweeple have discovered your twitterstream and like you. Think of it as hitting the Twitter jackpot for that day. See Followpalooza.

Friendscraping: This term is used when you start following a follower's followers. If you look at a follower's followers and find that a lot of them already follow you, then you have a good chance of having a high followback percentage if you follow them. This is usually a good way of getting followers. You can wait a few days and unfollow those who didn't followback.

FTL: For The Loss (abbreviation)

FTW: For The Win (abbreviation)

G

GAC: Get a Clue (abbreviation)

geolocation/geotagging (Tweet With Your Location): One option you have with your tweets is to send them with geolocation turned on. Then the location where you were when you tweeted will be available. Fortunately the default is for it to be turned off and you have to opt in to send your location with your tweets. If you are sending a 911 tweet make certain geolocation is turned on so they can find where you tweeted from.

geoTwitter: Location tracking of tweets.

ghost twitterer: Someone hired to tweet for someone else (usually for a celebrity or politician).co-twitterer is a similar term (see page 203).

GFF (Get Followers Fast): Sites that promise to get you followers if you sign onto their service. Usually they'll present you with something like a follower train. You can pay (and stay on the train longer) or join for free and make your way through the train faster, and get fewer followers. You follow everyone on a list and then your name is added to the list (at that back of the train) and someone else's is bumped off. Your name moves up the train until your name will be bumped. Eventually you'll be added again, only to be bumped again. For the most part these "train" sites aren't worth it. And the worst part is that you've given them authorization to use your Twitter account (that's how they can follow people as they move you up the train). And with that access you'll find they're sending a lot of spam from your account, and Twitter might suspend your account. Most of that spam is tweeting your endorsement of their Twitter train so more will sign up and hopefully pay to join it rather than use the free options. Stay away from any Twitter application/website that uses the word "train" to describe their services. It's a scam and your Twitter account will be spamming people and Twitter will suspend you.

GLHF: good luck have fun (abbreviation)

GM: good morning (abbreviation)

GR8: great (abbreviation)

H

hand: have a nice day (abbreviation)

Handle: Your [twitter_id]. This term derives from old CB Radio slang.

Hivemind: All the intelligence on Twitter collected into the collective unconscious, a hive mentality

HT, H/T (hat tip): This is another credit tag for something you retweet. This means not only are you retweeting but it's such a good tweet you're giving it a tip of your hat.

I

IC: I see (abbreviation)

ICYMI: in case you missed it (abbreviation)

IDK: i don't know (abbreviation)

illTwitterate: A newbie on Twitter. Someone who makes a lot of mistakes because they aren't certain what they're doing.

IM: Instant Message (abbreviation)

IMO: In My Opinion (abbreviation)

IMHO: In My Humble Opinion (abbreviation)

intwituation/intwituated: A Twitter infatuation.

IRL: in real life (abbreviation)

iTweet: A tweet from an iPhone or iPad.

J

JK j/k: just kidding (abbreviation)

JSYK: just so you know (abbreviation)

K

K: shortened form of okay (abbreviation)

KEYS: knock your socks off (abbreviation)

kk: shortened keel keel (cool cool) (abbreviation)

L

L8: late (abbreviation)

L8er: later (abbreviation)

Listed: Twitter has a listing option. If you have interesting tweets someone in addition to following you can keep you separate from everyone else they follow by putting you in a list they've created. For example if one of your interests is crocheting then someone interested in crocheting might follow you, but since they also follow tweeple interested in other things they might want to make a list of all the "crocheting" tweeple they follow. That way if they just want to see the tweets about crocheting amongst the tweeple they follow, then they can just click on their crocheting list. Being included in lists is a good thing and will increase your Twitter followers. Someone else might look at that crocheting list and decide to follow everyone on the list (hitting a single button). So, your name is on the list, and they will follow you and you'll pick up another follower. You can create as many lists as you want and be included in as many lists as twitterers want to include you.

LMK: let me know (abbreviation)

LOL: laughing out loud (abbreviation)

M

Micro-blogging: First there was blogging in which people wrote about what they were feeling, their hobbies, politics, religion, things they knew about, and even things they didn't know about. All with enormous authority at at great length. Then along came Twitter and people started doing the same thing only in 140-character tweets. If the first was called blogging, then the latter is micro-blogging. A lot of bloggers use Twitter to supplement their blog by mention the topic of a blog and then driving traffic to their blog by linking to it from Twitter. And there are some tweeple who feel uncomfortable with the wordiness of blogging, and for them micro-blogging on Twitter is the perfect solution for them.

MILT: Mother/mom I'd like to tweet (abbreviation)

mistweet: a tweet you regret after thinking about it. A high percentage of beertweets are also mistweets.

MT (modified tweet): A tweet that has to be modified in order to be retweeted. If you have the space it's good twitiquette to put MT in the tweet to let tweeple know it differs from the original. And if they know that and you've included the @[twitter_id] (also considered good twitiquette) of the original poster they can do a search to find the original tweet. Sometimes the modification is also to correct spelling/punctuation errors, link errors, etc. Cuttweet has a similar meaning (see page 203).

MRT (modified retweet): A retweet that has been further modified, usually to make it tweetable with the extra retweet information.

N

narcissitwit: A twitterer who tweets mainly about themself. Egotwistical is a similar term (see page 204).

newtweeter: A new twitterer just starting out on Twitter. Cut them some slack. You weren't always as awesome as you are now. Noobitwit (below) and Twewbie (see page 222) are similar terms.

nom nom nom: Represents eating/chewing with great enjoyment. You might tweet something like, "Having lunch right now. nom nom nom." That tells others you're enjoying it a lot.

noobitwit: A new twitterer just starting out on Twitter. Cut them some slack. You weren't always as awesome as you are now. Newtweeter (above) and Twewbie (see page 222) are similar terms.

NSFW: Not Safe For Work (abbreviation). This is used when you are including a link on your tweet to an article or picture that might not be appropriate to be viewed in the workplace. It's a head's up so the person clicking on the link won't accidentally open something inappropriate while the boss is walking by, and then have to try to come up with an explanation concerning what is visible on the screen. And many companies have software that keeps track of the files their employees open so they can find employees opening inappropriate files during working hours on company computers. If someone puts NSFW in their tweet, wait until you get home to open the link

nw: now watching (abbreviation). An abbreviation letting someone know that you're online and watching their tweets. Usually a rather benign comment, but if someone has been threatening you it might take on a more sinister meaning.

NTS: Not To Self (abbreviation)

O

OAuth: Twitter's login validation method that gives you the ability to grant a third party access to your account without you having to give them your login or password. You can rescind OAuth at any time in the settings section (see page 56).

occasionitter: Someone who tweets only occasionally and is not suffering from OCT (Obsessive Compulsive Twittering).

OCT: Obsessive Compulsive Twittering (abbreviation)

OH: overheard or other half (abbreviation). This is one of those abbreviations that has duel meanings, but the meanings are so different that you can easily discern whether it means overhear or other half just by the context of the tweet.

OMG: Oh my gosh/God (abbreviation)

otwituary: a Twitter obituary, someone's life in 140 characters. A lot of people will write otwituaries for historic dead people. Some are quite poignant, some are hilariously funny.

omnipotwit: An all knowing tweet. The final word on the matter.

P

peeps: Tweeple on Twitter. Derives from the term "peeps". A person's peeps are the tweeple who follow them in real life. Much as little chicks (peeps, from the peeping sounds they make) follow the mother chicken. Tweeps is a similar term (see page 221).

Phishing: Anything that tries to get you to give up your login/password information. Most often it's in the form of a fake email made to resemble a legitimate business. The email will warn you your account is going to be suspended if you don't re-register by filling out a form and sending it back. The form asks for your "user_id, password, location" at a minimum. Some are rather bold and ask for mother's maiden name, your city, telephone number, social security number. If anyone asks you for login information via an email forward that email to the company they supposedly represent. It'll turn out to be a phishing email.

pig twits: A term for tweets from a person whose huge fingers make it difficult for them to type accurately, so there are lots of mistakes in their tweets.

poetweet: A poem sent as a single tweet no longer than 140-characters.

poetweeter: A tweeter who writes poetweets.

politweet: A political tweet of not more than 140 characters.

politweeter: A political tweeter.

promoted tweets: These are tweets that appear at the top of Twitter search results because companies/individuals have paid to have their listing come before anyone else's. They can also appear in the sidebar as a promoted #hashtag:

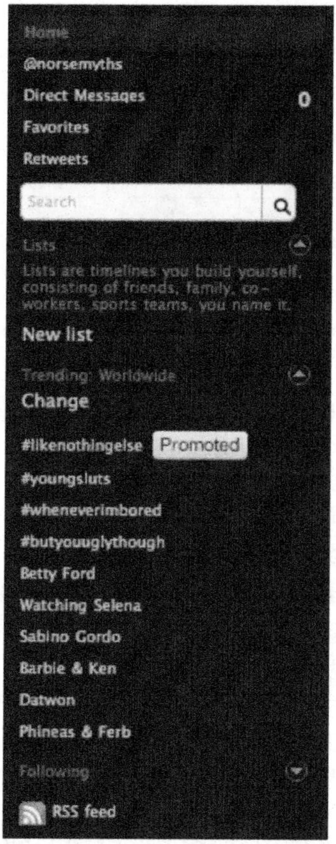

props: Stands for proper respect. Someone might give another twitterer props for their tweet as they retweet it. "Props to @[twitter_id]" for their excellent tweet.

PTR: Paying The Rent, a euphemism for going to the bathroom to do #2 (abbreviation)

pwincess: A princess on Twitter.

pwrty: A meetup of tweeple in real life.

Q

quid pro twuo: The Twitter version of quid pro quo (what for what). Essentially it means "You favorite my tweet and I'll favorite yours."

R

R: are (abbreviation)

rec: recommend (abbreviation)

repeatweet: A repeatweet is one you send again, usually at a different time of day to get a wider audience. Your audience in the morning on Twitter is probably different than your audience in the evening so they probably never saw your morning tweet. However, you do have to change the words a little. Twitter looks on duplicate tweets as spam and your second tweet will be flagged by Twitter as violating its TOS (Terms of Service). If you get flagged enough for sending out duplicate tweets your account can be suspended. The simple solution is to change a few words in your tweet. Or, if you're using a link shortener move the link to a different part of the tweet. Perhaps at the beginning of the tweet in the morning, and the end of the tweet in the evening. Or even make a new link which will make the tweet different. Or change to a different link shortener. Maybe goo.gl in the morning and bit.ly in the evening. That should be sufficient enough to avoid Twitter's ire. However, it seems that if you wait a couple of weeks you can send out the same tweet again (but only once in that new time period). Remember Twitter's search engine only goes back two weeks, and the same seems to be true for it's memory for duplicate tweets. A repeatweet is different from a retweet. Even though a retweet is identical to the original tweet, it is being sent from a different Twitter account. So a tweet can be retweeted any number of times by different twitterers. However, if it comes from your own account, only once every couple of weeks. You always want to keep Twitter happy. See threetweet, which is a similar term (see page 217).

reporTwitters: Tweeting reporters.

retweet (re-tweet), RT: If you like someone's tweet you might want to tweet it to your twitterstream. This is called retweeting. If you hover over their tweet the word "Retweet" will appear to the right of the tweet. Click on "Retweet" and a confirming message "Retweet to your followers?" will appear. You can click Yes to do so, or if you've changed your mind, you can hit the "x" to stop your retweet. You can also copy a tweet, hit "Home" in the top menu bar to bring up your twitterstream, type RT @[twitter_id) and hit paste, then send. The RT tells everyone you are retweeting; the @[twitter_id] tell whom you are retweeting; and the tweet tells you what you are retweeting. It is considered bad form to retweet someone's tweet without giving them credit. Sometimes adding the RT and the @[twitter_id] causes the tweet to go beyond the 140-character Twitter limit. In that instance you have to do some editing. The first thing you can do is shorten some words using accepted terms. Change "are" to "r", or "and" to "&". If that doesn't do it, then leave out punctuation, abbreviate words. Eventually you should be able to get the tweet to 140 characters. Unfortunately, that might mean another person wanting to retweet what you've retweeted might have even more problems getting to the 140-character limit because twitiquette is that they would also include your @[twitter_id] in the retweet of the retweet. However, in that instance if the only way to get to the 140-character limit is to leave off your @[twitter_id], then that's accepted.

RL: Real Life (abbreviation)

ROFL: Rolling on Floor Laughing

RT: Shortened form of retweet.

re-tweet: Another form of RT.

RTHX: Thanking someone for retreating your tweet.

RU: are you? (abbreviation)

S

Short code: the five-digit SMS (Short Message Service) account code used to send and receive text messages (usually 140-160 characters). In order to find the short code for your Twitter account go to this URL and follow the instructions:

https://support.twitter.com/articles/14226-how-to-find-your-twitter-short-code-or-long-code

sleet: A tweet in your sleep that you don't remember sending.

SMH: Shake My Head (abbreviation)

smore: Social Media Whore (abbreviation)

so tweet: Used to reference something that is cutely adorable, it is "oh, so tweet".

spam: Unwanted messages usually sent to promote a dubious product. The term derives from an old Monty Python sketch.

spatter: Another term for spam on Twitter.

speets: Spammy tweets.

styletweet: A tweet that's all about fashion or style.

super douchey: A tweet that has something in it that is truly annoying.

suspended account: Twitter will suspend your account if you violate their TOS (Terms of Service). So, don't do that.

sweeple: Very sweet tweeple.

spitter: A Twitter spammer.

T

Terms of Service (TOS): Twitter's rules of good behavior in order to maintain an active account. If you violate their TOS then Twitter will suspend your account.

T/J (Tweetjacking): Someone who takes someone else's tweet, puts their link to it and tweets it as if it's their own.

TFF: Twitter Friend Forever (abbreviation)

TFTT: Thanks for This Tweet (abbreviation)

threetweet: someone retweeting the same tweet for a third time. Repeatweet is a similar term (see page 216).

THX: thanks (abbreviation)

TIA: Thanks in Advance (abbreviation)

trabling: traveling to meet twitterers in real life.

tradspel: traditional spelling of a word in its own language.

trashtweeter: A trash talking twitterer.

TT: Trending Topic (abbreviation)

TTYL: Talk To You Later (abbreviation)

TTYS: Talk To You Soon (abbreviation)

twabe/twabes: Twitter babes, referencing women on Twitter and to be used affectionately, not in a derogatory manner. BTW women make up 64% of twitterers, men only 36%.

twabstinence: When one decides a little abstinence from Twitter is called for and takes a short break.

twabulous: A fabulous tweet on Twitter is simply twabulous.

twadd: A twadd is a Twitter add/follow.

twaddicted: Addicted to Twitter.

twaffic: Twitter traffic.

twaffle: A Twitter raffle. A twitterer might twaffle something off, but only to followers, which also makes it a way to get new followers.

twaggle: A Twitter gaggle of followers.

twaintenance: Regular maintenance of your Twitter account.

twaiting: Twittering while waiting around.

twake-up: Immediately tweeting when you wakeup before you even get out of bed.

twalker: Someone who pays particular attention to just one person on Twitter. Kinda like stalking.

twalking: Who says you can't tweet and walk at the same time? If you do you're twalking.

twallpaper: The wallpaper background on your Twitter page. Don't use any of the Twitter default wallpapers. There are much better available for free (see page 157).

twam: Spam on Twitter. Twammer is a similar term.

twamen: So be it. The equivalent of saying amen on Twitter.

twammer(s): A Twitter spammer(s).

twance: A Twitter dance. A lot of twitterers engaged in conversation with a series of tweets.

twander: When you start wandering amongst a twitterer's followers to their follower's to their followers, etc. You are wandering around the twitterverse.

twandle: Your [twitter_id], your handle. The term handle derives from CB radio.

twant: A rant on Twitter usually about politics.

twantrum: A Twitter tantrum resulting in lots of tweets.

twapp: Twitter apps.

twapplications: Twitter applications.

twappy: Means happy twittering away the time.

twardware: Twitter hardware, such as your cell phone.

twart: Twitter art. This can be simple ascii art, or a link to photographs/ art.

twasome: Something on Twitter that's awesome.

twasted: Someone who's wasted on Twitter, tweeting without stopping.

twatch, twatchin': Tweeting about a tv program while you're watching it. It can be very communal if others watching the show also join in with tweets and retweets.

twaunt: To taunt someone with tweets.

tweaching: Preaching through tweets, using scripture and sermons.

twedo: Fixing a tweet that might have a problem (misspelled word, incorrect link, etc.) and then retweeting it.

tweekend: What Saturday and Sunday are called when you do nothing all weekend but tweet.

tweeple, tweople: Twitter people. Your tweeps.

tweeps: Twitter people. Your tweeple. Derives its name from the term "peeps". A person's peeps are the tweeple who follow them in real life.

Much as little chicks (peeps, from the peeping sounds they make) follow the mother chicken. Peeps is a similar term (see page 214).

tweet: A Twitter post. Without tweets there would be no Twitter.

TYL: Tweet You Later. What you say when you've finished tweeting for a while and decide to go do something else possibly in real life or on facebook.

tweetaholic: Someone with a real Twitter addiction problem.

tweetaholism: A Twitter addiction seriously in need of a 12-step program.

tweetback (tweet-back): When you refer to a previous tweet in a new tweet.

tweeted: Past tense of tweet.

tweeter: Someone who uses Twitter and sends out tweets. Used interchangeably with twitterer.

tweetheart: Your special friend on Twitter, your tweeple sweetheart.

tweeting: The act of posting tweets on Twitter.

tweets: Short 140-character messages posted on Twitter.

tweetup: A real world/real life meet up of tweeters. Yes, people do exist in flesh and blood.

tweepleworld: The world of Twitter. Twitosphere (see page 221) and twitterverse (see page 224) are similar terms.

twetiquette (twitiquette): The rules of courtesy on Twitter. Etiquette rules for Twitter.

twewbie: A new twitterer just starting out on Twitter. Cut them some slack. You weren't always as awesome as you are now. Twewbie derives from the term newbie, which was first applied to AOL (America OnLine) members logging onto the internet usually for the first time. They tended to be not quite computer literate or sophisticated in their usage or comments. Who is in the beginning?. But there were so many AOLers logging on and making mistakes in chatrooms, and being constantly corrected in forums the phrase, "Don't yell at me I'm only a newbie" became attached to them. Calling someone a newbie at that time was an insult and considered derogatory. Newtweeter (see page 212) and Noobitwit (see page 212) are similar terms.

twexercising: Tweeting while at the gym on a spinbike, stairstepper, etc.

twexican: A Mexican twitterer.

twexit: You make your twexit when you're finally finished with Twitter for the day and tell everyone you'll be gone for awhile but will BBL.

twhiner: A whining twitterer whose tweets have taken on a definite whine.

twibe: A group of twitterers with a common interest. You can be the member of more than one twibe.

twitamin: A short tweet about health.

twitbud: A Twitter buddy.

twitch: Tweeting almost as a responsive twitch.

twitiquette (twetiquette): The rules of courtesy on Twitter. Etiquette rules for Twitter.

twitosphere: The blogosphere of twitterers. Tweepleworld (see page 222) and twitterverse (see page 224).

Twitter client: Third party software or websites that let you send tweets. Some let you tweet ahead/schedule future tweets (Dynamic Tweets, see page 151). Others let you tweet from your iPhone, Android Phone, Blackberry, or SmartPhone.

Twitter lists: This Twitter feature gives you the ability to create multiple lists of favorite tweeple, topics, or interests. Just click on the "List" button above the start of your twitterstream. The dropdown menu gives you the options of managing your lists. You can create a new list, add to a list, or delete a list. Lists are a great way of organizing your interests. And other tweeple can see your lists, and also see how many lists you are included in.

Twitter search: Twitter has hundreds of millions of subscribers and you can do a Twitter search through all those subscribers to find tweeple interested in what you're interested in, or talking about topics you're interested in. Click on "Find people" in the top menu bar to search for specific people. But this is very limiting. If you type in "search.Twitter.com" in the URL field in your browser Twitter's search field comes up. You can then search by name, places, people, trending topics, events, etc. Once you hit the search button the search.Twitter.com and the search criteria form a URL in your URL browser field. You can drag this URL into your bookmarks bar (or save it in your bookmarks) so that anytime you want to do that search with that criteria you can just hit the URL in your bookmarks bar or in your bookmarks folder. If you are searching from a Twitter client, many of them give you the option of saving your searches. One search you should save is a search with your [twitter_id]. When you search for yourself you bring up not only your recent tweets, retweets, replies and DM's, you also bring up the tweeple who have repleid to you, commented about you, or retweeted you.

twitterer: Someone who uses Twitter and sends out tweets. Used interchangeably with tweeter.

twittering: Using Twitter.

twitterings: tweets

twitterverse: The universe of Twitter. Tweepleworld (see page 222) and Twitosphere (see page 223).

U

U: you (abbreviation)

unfollow: If you tire of someone's tweets or are maybe offended by something they've tweeted you can unfollow them from their twitterstream by clicking on their [twitter_id] (or typing Twitter.com/[twitter_id] in the URL browser field). When their twitterstream comes up you'll see a gear button next to the Lists button at the top right of their stream. Click on the gear and you'll get a drop-down menu that gives you options to: Mention, Unfollow, Block, Report. Choose Unfollow to unfollow them. If they are following you they might notice you've unfollowed them and unfollow you. They might also be using a Twitter client (or website) that automatically unfollows those who unfollow them. So, you do take a risk when you unfollow someone of losing that person as a follower.

V

via: When you retweet someone's tweet, or even refer to what someone has mentioned in a tweet it is considered good twitiquette to do a via @[twitter_id] with your tweet to give them credit. See also hat-tip or h/t.

W

w w/: with (abbreviation)

w/e: weekend (abbreviation)

w00t: woohoo (abbreviation)

wazzup/whaddup: What's up?

WGACA: What Goes Around Comes Around (abbreviation)

white-listed: Accounts that are allowed to exceed Twitter's limits. These are accounts that are building api's that need to exceed Twitter's limits. If they're offering a service to twitterers to follow, unfollow, or search on Twitter and they have more than one client, then they could easily exceed Twitter's limits, making the service their offering unworkable. They can apply to Twitter and convince Twitter that letting their product exceed api limits is somehow beneficial to Twitter.

whoot: Yay! Woohoo!

wld: would (abbreviation)

widget: a piece of code that can be inserted in websites to add some sort of functionality. Twitter offers several badge widgets.

wzup: What's up? (abbreviation)

X

Y

YKWIM: you know what I mean (abbreviation)

YOYO: you're own your own (abbreviation)

YW: You're welcome (abbreviation)

Z

SMILEYS

ORIGINAL SMILEY

original smiley :-)

ANIMAL

butterfly }|{

butterfly })i({

cat }:-X

cat >^,,^<

chicken 8^

cow 3:-o

dog :3-]

dog <(-'.'-)>

fish <:))><

fish (caught) ----------<;))><

frog 8)

koala @(*0*)@

orangutan (:=)

penguin 8>

pig :8)

APPEARANCE

has a cold (runny nose) :-~)

broken nose (:^(

messy hair #:-)

<table>
<tr><td>double chin</td><td>:-))</td></tr>
<tr><td>CRYING AND SAD</td><td></td></tr>
<tr><td>frowning</td><td>(:(</td></tr>
<tr><td>sad</td><td>:-(</td></tr>
<tr><td>sad</td><td>(:-(</td></tr>
<tr><td>sad</td><td>(:-\</td></tr>
<tr><td>crying</td><td>:’(</td></tr>
<tr><td>crying</td><td>:’-(</td></tr>
<tr><td>crying</td><td>:`-(</td></tr>
<tr><td>crying</td><td>;-(</td></tr>
<tr><td>crying</td><td>:~(</td></tr>
<tr><td>crying smiley</td><td>:~-(</td></tr>
<tr><td>EXPRESSIONS</td><td></td></tr>
<tr><td>blank Expression</td><td>(:-</td></tr>
<tr><td>skeptical</td><td>:-/</td></tr>
<tr><td>one eyebrow raised</td><td>`:-)</td></tr>
<tr><td>up all night</td><td>%-)</td></tr>
<tr><td>up all night</td><td>%-|</td></tr>
<tr><td>screaming</td><td>:-@</td></tr>
<tr><td>cursing</td><td>:-@!</td></tr>
<tr><td>you’re kidding?</td><td>(@@)</td></tr>
<tr><td>OMG</td><td>8-O</td></tr>
<tr><td>yawning</td><td>I-O</td></tr>
<tr><td>talkative</td><td>:-0</td></tr>
</table>

yelling   :-(0)

whatever   ]:->

FLOWERS AND TREES

flower   *->--

flower (long stemmed)   *->----

rose with thorns   @-,-'--

rose with thorns   @-'-,--

rose   @>--->---

Christmas Tree   *<<<<+

FULL FIGURE

man   O>-<

woman   O>-<|=

hands up!   (:>-<

man   :-(<|

pregnant woman   :-|8()

hugs   {{hugs}}

hugs   (((H)))

giggles   /\/\/\

ITEMS

heart   <3

sword   --{----

feather (just teasing), tickling   ->>>>>--

MESSAGES

I live in an apartment complex	[][][][][]
sleeping	ZZzzZZzzZZzzZZzz
SOS (actual)	...---...

MIDGET SMILEYS

frowning	:(
crying	;(
real downer	:[
undecided	:\
What's going on?	?)
singing	:O
my lips are sealed	-#
tongue hanging out in anticipation	-P
sticking out tongue	:P
wearing glasses	8)

MISCELLANEOUS

baby	~:o
vampire	:-[
Pinnochio	:---)
dead smiley (possibly suicide)	X-(
kissing smiley	(:-*
my lips are sealed	:-#
mooning everyone	(00)

TALKING, MOUTHS

sticking its tongue out of the right side of its mouth	:-b
sticking its tongue out	:-P
sticking its tongue out (profile)	.'P
Grinning sticking tongue out. Tongue is a Latin Capital Thorn Unicode U+00DE UTF8: C3 9E HTML &THORN Decimal: Þ Hex: Þ)	:oÞ
Grinning sticking tongue out. Tongue is a Latin Small Letter Thorn Unicode U+00FE UTF8: C3 BE HTML &thorn Decimal: þ Hex: þ)	:oþ
talking out of side of mouth	:-7
tongue in cheek	:-?
blabber mouth	(:-D
laughing at you!	:-D

orator	**:-0**
surprised	**:-o**
loud shouting	**:-O**
totally incredulous	**:-C**

WEARING GLASSES

wearing glasses	**B-)**
wearing glasses	**8=)**
wearing glasses	**(8-)**

WEARING SOMETHING ON THEIR HEAD

angel with halo	**O:-)**
angel with halo	**O :-)**
angel with halo	**0:-)**
angel with halo	**O:)**
angel with halo winking	**0;-)**
baseball cap	**d:)**
baseball cap	**d:-)**
beret	**/:-)**
chef	**C=:-)**
chef	**8=:-)**
dunce	**<:-I**
clown	***<):o)**
party hat	***<8-)**
party, bow tie	***<8-)X**
earphones	**[:-)**

football player	C:#

WINKING

winking	;-)
one eye wink	,-)
one eye wink	‘-)
pirate	P-)
smiley with one eyebrow raised	,:-)
It’s all fun and games until a smiley gets its eye poked out	.-(

Printed in Dunstable, United Kingdom

91221341R00147